Can India grow without *Bharat*?

SHANKAR ACHARYA is one of India's leading policy economists. As Chief Economic Adviser to the Government of India (1993-2000) he was deeply involved in the economic reforms of the 1990s. He also served on the Securities and Exchange Board of India (SEBI) and, more recently, as Member, Twelfth Finance Commission (2004). He has authored several books and numerous scholarly articles.

Currently he is Honorary Professor and Board Member of the Indian Council for Research on International Economic Relations (ICRIER), New Delhi. He also serves on the governing boards of other national research organisations (including NCAER and NIPFP) and various advisory bodies of Government, the Reserve Bank and some corporates. He writes regularly in the *Business Standard* and is a consultant to international organisations. Dr. Acharya has a Ph.D from Harvard University and a B.A. from Oxford.

Can India grow without *Bharat*?

'Columnspeak'

SHANKAR ACHARYA

ACADEMIC FOUNDATION
NEW DELHI

Published in 2007
by: ACADEMIC FOUNDATION
4772-73 / 23 Bharat Ram Road, (23 Ansari Road),
Darya Ganj, New Delhi - 110 002 (India).
Tel: 23245001 / 02 / 03 / 04.
Fax: +91-11-23245005.
E-mail: academic@vsnl.com
www.academicfoundation.com

Can India grow without Bharat?
by Shankar Acharya

ISBN-13: 978-81-7188-615-9
ISBN-10: 81-7188-615-9

Designed and typeset by Italics India, New Delhi.
Printed and bound in India.

10 9 8 7 6 5 4 3 2 1

To my readers

CONTENTS

D. Economic growth

E. Infrastructure problems

F. Budget and tax policies

G. Foreign trade and payments

H. Monetary and fiscal policies

I. Foreign affairs

Preface

With the exception of the first (which appeared in *Outlook*), all these essays appeared in the *Business Standard* over the past three years*. The title of this volume is taken from one of the earliest columns (November 2003). The reason for doing so is that the essay highlights the two greatest challenges confronting India's economic and social development in the next two decades or so. These are the challenge of providing productive employment opportunities for the country's burgeoning labour force and the (associated) challenge of rising disparities in incomes and opportunities across states, regions and people of India.

Over these past three years or so there has been much euphoria about both India's recent growth performance and her long-term potential as an emerging economic superpower. Much of this optimism rests on the demographics of India's youthful population and its enormous potential for growth as the share of working age population continues to rise for the next 30 years or more. In this and other essays I emphasise repeatedly that the demographics simply promise a rapidly increasing 'supply' of labour. Successful long-term development will depend crucially on an equally rapid expansion of job opportunities, that is, the 'demand' for labour. Our past record is much less reassuring on this prospect. Growth

* See "Sources" at the back of book for publication dates of each article.

may have been rapid but the decline in poverty has been slow (the poverty head count ratio has only fallen from 26 to 22 per cent in the five years between 1999/00 and 2004/05). This is because the crucial transmission mechanism between growth and poverty alleviation (namely, rapid employment growth in labour-using manufacturing and services) has been blunted in India by a number of factors, including complex and rigid labour laws, small-scale industry reservations, bad infrastructure and poor education policies and programmes.

Partly for this reason and partly because the bulk of India's increase in population and labour force is occurring (and will continue to do so in the next four decades) in a handful of weakly governed, populous, poor and slow-growing states (such as Uttar Pradesh, Bihar, Madhya Pradesh and Orissa), disparities are on the rise: between advanced and backward states; between a few million graduates with marketable skills and the hundreds of millions of semi-educated school-leavers and dropouts; and between the 27 million organised sector workers (including all levels of government) with protected jobs and nearly 400 million unorganised sector workers, toiling for little remuneration and even less security.

The essays in this Section B (as well as C, D and E) discuss and outline the key reforms required to promote faster growth of employment and output. Those in Section C dwell on the halting progress in economic reforms, especially since the advent of the UPA government and despite its much vaunted 'dream team' of top economic managers (Prime Minister Manmohan Singh, Finance Minister P. Chidambaram and Planning Commission Deputy Chairman, Montek Ahluwalia). These essays highlight the baneful influence of bad economic ideas embedded in the National Common Minimum Programme and trace their consequences in populist programmes and policies.

Despite such policies and sluggish economic reforms, economic growth has averaged 8 per cent in the four years after 2002/03, fuelling expectations that the Indian economy is firmly on a 8 per cent plus long-term growth trajectory. The essays in Section D cast doubt on such projections, pointing to the strong cyclical component of the recent dynamism and emphasising the major policy shortcomings and constraints in agriculture, labour policies, infrastructure (further elaborated in Section E), fiscal management, education and health policies and the 'drag' of a still large and inefficient public sector in energy, banking and transport.

Section F consists of appraisals of budgets (from 2004 onwards) and tax policies. They show that these policies have been a mixed bag, with both good and bad initiatives. Foreign trade and payments issues are analysed in Section G, including critiques of the newfound love for bilateral and regional trade agreements and of a somewhat fanciful aspiration for a common currency for SAARC. Section H offers analyses of monetary and fiscal policies and warns against any complacency on fiscal deficits, especially given the past correlation between rising fiscal deficits and slowing growth.

The last group of essays stray outside the realm of pure economics and consider some foreign policy issues, including two on China-India as well as a recent, favorable appraisal of the UPA government's foreign policies in its first two and a half years in office.

In closing, I want to warmly thank the *Business Standard* and *Outlook* magazine for permission to include in this volume columns, which originally appeared in these journals. I also wish to thank the Academic Foundation for their speedy and professional work in bringing out this small volume of short essays. In particular, I am indebted to Rituraj Kapila for his unfailing courtesy and high order of professionalism. Last, but by no means least, I am grateful to my readers who have consistently rewarded my journalistic forays with warm feedback and, occasionally, friendly and welcome criticism.

A

India: then and now

1

India's economy: then and now

The last 15 years have witnessed tremendous changes in Indian economic policies and performance. The ramparts erected in the previous 40 years (1950-1990) against foreign trade, capital flows and technology have been largely dismantled and the winds of globalisation are sweeping across this ancient and tradition-bound land. The hitherto unquestioned primacy of the government and public sector in economic development has been challenged. The 'licence-permit *raj*' has been weakened, but by no means eliminated. The results have been salutary. Economic growth has accelerated. Urbanisation has gathered momentum. Poverty has declined. Foreign trade has expanded. Indian industry has renewed its vigour in the fires of open competition. India's services sector has burgeoned and parts of it (IT and BPO) have achieved international excellence and recognition. Whether all of India is shining or not, a newly affluent urban middle class is flaunting its confidence.

What happened? Why? Are we really becoming a big economic power? What does the future hold for this nation of 1.1 billion (and growing) in the decade ahead? Let's explore the contours of this exciting story.

Not so long ago (1990), in a country far, far away, foreign commerce was severely repressed. Exports were discouraged by an overvalued exchange rate (Rs. 18 per US dollar), hideously complex access to imported inputs and low profitability compared to the hugely protected domestic market. Imports were controlled through detailed licensing of almost all products and unbelievably high customs duties ('peak' rates were higher than 200 per cent!). An equally Kafkaesque system of industrial licensing told entrepreneurs and manufactures what to produce, where and how much! Banks (overwhelmingly, government owned) were told how to give credit, at what rates, how much and to whom. All interest rates were set by government and the Reserve Bank. Needless to say, there was a flourishing illegal market of bribes and pay-offs for most licences and permits, which was intimately entwined with politics and election finance. Forex control (and scarcity) was the reigning deity to which all public policy paid homage, while the 'hawala' trade flourished. Predictably, there were hardly any private inflows of foreign investment.

What else can we remember about 1990? Well, there were only three makes of cars, the Ambassador, the Premier Padmini and the 'new' Maruti-Suzuki. Indica was a good name for an encyclopaedia. Television pretty much meant Doordarshan. Nobody had heard of Infosys and Wipro, let alone Narayanmurthy and Premji. The World-Wide-Web suggested a horror movie on spiders. Jet referred to a type of aircraft, not an airline (which didn't exist). 'Nifty' meant swift, not a stock exchange index, since the NSE was only created in 1994. The term 'FII' didn't mean anything; the policy which birthed foreign institutional investors came in late 1992. Foreign trips were only taken by the very rich and government officials, who were usually burdened with shopping lists by spouses, relatives and friends for consumer 'goodies' (including quality razor blades, cosmetics and ball point pens) not available in the country. Telephone connections came with your job…or you waited a few years! Cell phones didn't exist.

On to this overregulated, inward-looking, underperforming economy was grafted the fiscal profligacy of the late 1980s and the temporary oil shock of the first Iraq (Kuwaiti) war. The result was the full-fledged external payments crisis of 1991, with industrial growth falling, inflation soaring and the overall economy stagnating. The new Congress government might have responded with harsher controls on foreign trade and payments. Instead, Prime

Minister Narasimha Rao appointed a technocratic finance minister and gave him strong political backing. The rest is history. Manmohan Singh and his small band of reforming colleagues (including Montek Ahluwalia, P. Chidambaram and C. Rangarajan) launched an array of reforms, which changed the course of India's economic history. The exchange rate was devalued and made market-responsive. Industrial licensing was swept away, as was much of import licensing. Customs duties were sharply reduced and other taxes reformed. Foreign direct and portfolio foreign investment were welcomed. The fiscal deficit was cut. Interest rates were freed. Banking was reformed (partially) and the stock market was modernised, including, by establishing the electronic-trade-based NSE and giving SEBI legal backing.

The fruits of the ongoing reform programme were reaped very swiftly. Economic growth surged to exceed 7 per cent in three successive years in the mid-nineties. Industrial growth leapt to double digits. Agriculture recorded the fastest 5-year growth (1992-1997) in India's history at 4.7 per cent. Exports grew at 20 per cent for three consecutive years. Remittances from NRIs quadrupled in four years and foreign investment went from negligible to $ 5 billion in the same period, taking foreign currency reserves from $ 2 to $ 20 billion in short order. Stock prices recovered from the 1992 scam and new issues flourished. New private banks were launched.

Although the momentum of reforms slowed after 1995, the broad direction of change in favour of greater market orientation and more private sector participation remained intact. Despite successive changes of government, disinvestment of public enterprises continued, the telecom sector was opened up and so were domestic airlines and insurance. There was more hesitant progress in electric power, ports and roads. Private television channels mushroomed. Capital markets were strengthened. Remaining import licensing was phased out by 2001 and peak customs duties steadily reduced (down to 15 per cent in the recent budget). Given the three changes in government at the centre since 1995, the continuity in policies is remarkable.

The cumulative impact of the initial reforms and the more sporadic initiatives since has been enormous. Economic growth has averaged 6.2 per cent since 1991, making India one of the 10 fastest growing countries in the world. Today, average living standards are 70 per cent higher than in 1991, having clocked average growth at 4.3 per cent a year for 13 years. Literacy increased from 52 to 66 per cent of the population. According to the NCAER, almost 100 million people now live in households with incomes between Rs. 2 to 10 lakhs a year, compared to around 15 million in 1991. This is India's rising middle class. The proportion of people below the poverty line has dropped from nearly 40 per cent to around 20 per cent. Exports of goods and services (including remittances) now account for 20 per cent of GDP as compared to 10 per cent in 1991. Annual software exports have risen from near zero to $ 17 billion, while foreign investment has climbed from barely $ 100 million to over $ 16 billion, thanks mainly to the spurt in FII investments in our stock market. With forex reserves at $ 135 billion the problem today is managing their abundance! Annual sales of two-wheelers have tripled from 1.8 million in 1991 to 5.6 million in 2004, while those of cars (plus SUVs) have soared from two lakhs to a million. Fixed telephone connections rose from 5 to 45 million in 13 years, while mobiles jumped from 2 to 50 million in the past 4 years.

Not everything is hunky-dory. Over two hundred million Indians still live—barely—in abject poverty, below a minimal poverty line. More than three-fourths of them are in rural India, where the annual growth of agriculture has slumped to hardly 2 per cent since 1997. Shockingly, almost half of India's children under 5 were undernourished in 2001 (compared to 12 per cent in China). And 46 per cent of India's female population was illiterate (only 5 per cent in China). Over 40 million job-seekers were registered with employment exchanges in 2004, while employment in the organised sector (including government) of the economy stagnated below 30 million throughout the last 13 years. Unsurprisingly, India is ranked at a lowly 127th out of 177 countries by the latest UNDP index of human development. Improvement is unlikely to be swift, given the pressures on state finances and the continuing decline in governance and administrative capacities. The geographic pattern of India's development has remained skewed, with the populous central and eastern states of Uttar Pradesh, Madhya Pradesh, Bihar, Jharkand and Orissa, lagging behind the rest of the country. In 2002, average income in Bihar was less than one quarter of levels in rich states like Haryana, Punjab and Maharashtra! The poor quality of our physical infrastructure (especially, power, roads, ports and water supply) is well-known. Large fiscal deficits (10 per cent of GDP for centre and states) soak up private savings and bloat government debt. Above all, the old mindset of government interventionism, subsidies and patronage is still influential, especially in predominantly government-owned sectors of energy, banking, transport, power and water.

While our engagement with the world economy has increased substantially since 1991, we are still far from being a serious economic power in global trade and finance. Our share of world goods exports may have doubled since 1991 from 0.4 to 0.8 per cent in 2004. But it pales in comparison to China's surge from 2 per cent share to over 6 per cent in the same period. In each of the last three years, the increase in China's foreign trade has exceeded India's total foreign trade! In the last quarter of a century, foreign direct investment into China has cumulated to a staggering $ 560 billion. Over the same period, India has received hardly $ 35 billion, less than the $ 60 billion that poured into China in 2004 alone. If only our Left parties would emulate China's example towards globalisation! A tragic result of our timid approach to global economic opportunities (coupled with rigid labour laws, small-scale industry reservation policy and bad infrastructure) has been the slow growth of our industrial output and employment. In 2003, there were hardly 5 million workers in organised manufacturing out of a labour force of over 350 million! In contrast, Chinese factories employed over 100 million workers.

Bottom line: we have come a long way from 1990 but we have a long, long way to go. What does the future hold for us? Our potential is enormous. We are the only big country where the proportion of working age people in total population will continue to increase for the next 30 years. So there should be no shortage of workers or savings. Our industry has demonstrated its capacity to compete effectively in an increasingly open economy, despite the handicaps of infrastructure and bad policies. The new strengths in a widening variety of services promises much. India's capital markets have matured and shown the ability to attract large volumes of global funds, helped greatly by the high quality of many companies, some of which have listed in New York and London exchanges. Our democracy may be messy and contentious, but it is deep-rooted and assures stability and peaceful changes in government.

Even cautious conservatives (like me) expect India's economic growth to average 6 per cent a year over the next decade, barring a major crisis in banking, public finances or the world economy. Bolder optimists foresee 8 per cent growth. The difference may appear small, but in per capita terms it's the difference between 4.5 and 6.5 per cent. Under the former, average living standards will improve 55 per cent by 2015. With the latter, they will almost double.

Economic growth at 8 per cent is possible. But it requires major reforms in at least five important areas. First, if we are to really utilise our abundant resource of labour to accelerate economic expansion, then we must reform our labour laws, which hugely discourage new employment and investment in organised industry. Otherwise, the demographic dividend of an expanding workforce could turn into an unemployment nightmare. Second, our sluggish agriculture (which provides livelihood to 60 per cent of our workforce) must be revitalised through more rural infrastructure (and less subsidies), greater diversification, removal of internal trade barriers and viable water policies. Third, the pervasive infrastructure bottlenecks must be broken (especially, in power) through serious policy changes and restructured government spending. Fourth, the massive government revenue deficits or dissaving (to the tune of 6 per cent of GDP) must be reduced to accommodate higher investment in the economy. Finally, we must privatise many government enterprises in energy, banking, transport and communications. It's the best way to spur greater productivity and competition.

If our governments do all this, then the Indian economy may well grow at 8 per cent over the next decade. This will take India's share of World GDP (measured at internationally comparable prices, or PPP) from the current 6 per cent to nearly 10 per cent. That would make us a serious economic power (China's share today is 12 per cent). Otherwise, as Lord Meghnad Desai has said, India may have to rest content with being a 'Great Democracy', while China becomes a truly 'Great Power'.

B

The employment challenge

2

Can India grow without *Bharat?*

The past couple of months have seen a resurgence of growth optimism about the Indian economy. In the short-run of the current fiscal year this is entirely justified by the exceptionally strong monsoon (following on the mini-drought of 2002/03), a mild cyclical upturn in industry and steady growth in services. The Indian economy could well grow at seven per cent or higher in 2003/04. But the growth optimism seems to extend well beyond the present year. A growing number of writers (including Vijay Kelkar and N.K. Singh) have emphasised the potential of some medium and long-term drivers of growth. In particular, they have pointed to the 'demographic dividend' generated by India's relatively youthful population, swelling the ranks of the labour force in the coming decades and reducing the dependency ratio of children plus senior citizens. Long-term optimism has also been fed by the recent Goldman Sachs study (*Dreaming with BRICs*), which projects the rising global economic role of Brazil, Russia, India and China in the next half century. Is such optimism justified? Are we really on a growth escalator which will lift India to the front rank of global economic powers in the next three to four decades?

In some ways the BRICs projections are most alluring from an Indian perspective. The study notes, "India has the potential to show the fastest growth over the next 30 and 50 years." What is really seductive is that the projections appear so modest and reasonable. India is seen to grow at about 6 per cent per year between now and 2040 and then slow down gradually to 5 per cent by 2050. None of the wishful 8 per cent of the Tenth Plan is invoked. And yet, even with such 'modest' growth, India attains today's Korean (RoK) standards of living by 2042 and Italy's (almost) by 2050. In terms of GDP in US dollars, the Indian economy would overtake UK in 20 years and Japan in 30 years! Such is the power of compound interest and a large base population. This is heady stuff. Should we just book our seat and enjoy the ride to *nirvana*? But perhaps we need to take a closer look first. What's driving this stellar long-term performance? The 'demographic dividend' seems to be a large part of this captivating tale. To quote: "Demographics play an important role in the way the world will change...With the only population out of the BRICs that continues to grow throughout the next 50 years, India has the potential to raise its US dollar income per capita to 35 times current levels." That's an increase of 3500 per cent!

What is this magic potion of 'demo-div'? It's part of the larger story of the 'demographic transition', which runs roughly as follows. In undeveloped economies both birth rates and death rates are high and, as a result, the population is static and poor. With development comes, advances in public health and disease control, which bring down the death rate. Since, initially, the birth rate stays high, population grows apace and, after a 10-15 year lag, so does the labour force. As development proceeds and technology improves, living standards rise and families prefer fewer children. Increasingly, they acquire the means to execute such aspirations. In short, the birth rate also starts to decline, leading to lower population growth. That, in turn, reduces labour force growth. That is the demographic transition of a society from high rates of birth and death to low ones. Towards the last third of this story, comes a phase (of several decades) when labour force growth is high (because of earlier births) but the proportion of dependent children is low (because of reduced birth rates). These are the decades when the economy has the highest proportion of its population in the working age (15-60) and offers the maximum potential for productive employment and growth. That's the demographic dividend.

Note one absolutely crucial point. The 'demo-div' is all about the 'supply' of labour. Nothing is said about 'demand.' Therein lies the catch. The additional labour supply offers the 'potential' for employment and growth. In a well-functioning economy with competitive product and factor markets labour demand would match supply and lead to more jobs and output. But there is no 'guarantee' of such a happy outcome. It all depends on how well the economy is run; in particular, how well labour markets work. Let's return to the reality of India. Between 1993/94 and 1999/00 the economy grew at over 6.5 per cent per year. But, according to the Tenth Plan, employment grew only 1 per cent per annum! This was a period when labour force was growing at over 2 per cent a year and there was plenty of backlog of underemployment and unemployment. Quite clearly, labour demand was growing far slower than labour supply. The labour market was far from perfect. There were many reasons. An important one is our rigid labour laws, which effectively convert labour from a variable to a fixed factor of production. Employers have every reason to avoid hiring new workers, knowing it is almost impossible to lay off workers in a downturn. In sharp contrast, firms in China employ millions of new workers each year knowing that they can be laid off if business conditions worsen. Of course, with capital surging in to avail of cheap, productive labour, the downturn never comes!

Another crucial point is that India's demographic trajectory is an average of the demographic paths of its constituent states. From around 1970, the fertility story has diverged considerably across states. For various reasons (including female education, gender parity, and improving incomes) Kerala led the way with rapid decline in fertility, followed by Tamil Nadu and other southern states and, subsequently, other states. By 1995, fertility rates (average live births per woman) in Kerala and Tamil Nadu had dropped below replacement level (2.1), other southern states and Maharashta had fertility levels below 3, another group of states had fertility levels between 3 and 4, while the BIMARU states (undivided) and Haryana still had rates above 4. In a recent EPW paper, Leela and Pravin Visaria have presented long-term population projections for these three groups of states. These are shown in Table 2.1 along with data on recent per capita incomes and state GDP growth. What do the data show?

First, the four BIMARU states have low per capita incomes (averaging below Rs. 10,000 per year) compared to the five low-fertility leaders in the demographic transition which average over Rs. 18,000. Second, the BIMARU economies have grown at only 4.6 per cent over the last decade compared to the 6.3 per cent clocked by the low-fertility states. The disparity is greater in terms of per capita income growth since population in BIMARU states has grown faster. Third, precisely because the BIMARU states are laggards in the demographic transition, they will see the highest relative and absolute expansion in population and labour force between now and 2051. Their share of India's population will rise from 41 per cent to 48 per cent, since nearly 60 per cent of India's population increment will be concentrated in these four states. In a nutshell, the 'demo-div' of a transitional labour supply bulge will be focussed on four populous, poor, slow-growing northern states, with weak infrastructure, education systems and governance. The chances of translating this 'potential' of additional labour supply into a 'reality' of employment and high growth, appear slim.

Returning to the BRICs study, the authors tested their projection model by running it 'backwards' for the period 1960-2000 for 11 countries. The 'predictions' were excellent—except for India, where the model 'predicted' growth of 7.5 per cent but the actual outcome was 4.5 per cent! Perhaps we shouldn't yet bank on this escalator to *nirvana*?

Table 2.1

Income, growth and population: major states

States	*Per capita NDP, 1999/00 at current prices (Rs. thousand)*	*GSDP Growth 1992-2002 (per cent per year)*	*Per cent of India's population*			*Population increment 2001-2051 (millions)*
			1971	*2001*	*2051*	
			Low fertility			
Kerala	18.3	6.1	3.9	3.1	2.2	4.2
Tamil Nadu	19.1	6.7	7.5	6.0	4.4	9.9
Andhra Pradesh	14.7	5.0	7.9	7.4	7.4	44.2
Karnataka	16.3	6.7	5.3	5.1	4.8	25.3
Maharashtra	23.4	6.8	9.2	9.4	9.1	50.6
Sub-total			***33.9***	***31.1***	***28.0***	***134.2***
			Medium fertility			
Punjab	23.0	4.6	2.5	2.4	2.2	11.4
West Bengal	15.6	6.6	8.1	7.8	7.5	41.7
Gujarat	18.6	8.2	4.9	4.9	4.5	22.4
Orissa	9.2	3.6	4.0	3.6	3.3	17.2
Assam	9.6	2.5	2.7	2.6	2.6	15.4
Sub-total			***22.1***	***21.3***	***20.2***	***108.1***
			High fertility			
Haryana	21.1	4.7	1.8	2.1	2.5	20.0
Madhya Pradesh	10.9	5.2	7.6	7.9	9.1	66.8
Bihar	6.3	3.1	10.3	10.7	11.6	78.2
Rajasthan	12.5	5.5	4.7	5.5	6.6	49.6
Uttar Pradesh	9.8	4.5	16.1	17.0	20.8	162.5
Sub-total			***40.5***	***43.1***	***50.6***	***377.1***
India	**15.6**	**6.0**	**100.0**	**100.0**	**100.0**	**619.4**

Source: *Economic Survey (2001/02)*; Tenth Five Year Plan, and Visaria, Leela and Pravin Visaria (2003)."Long Term Population Projections for Major States, 1991-2101", *Economic & Political Weekly*, November. Data are for undivided UP, MP and Bihar.

3

Guaranteeing employment or fiscal crisis?

Populism is abroad in the land. Free power for farmers is back. Subsidies on kerosene and LPG have increased. Special expenditure packages for particular states have been given. Price restraints on energy, steel and drugs seem back in vogue. Public sector bank employees have got hefty wage increases. Schemes for debt write-offs are bandied about. The list grows by the week. And this despite many decades of development experience that clearly shows that populist policies cannot achieve rapid and sustained growth of incomes and employment for a country. On the contrary, such policies generally retard growth and poverty alleviation.

Perhaps, the biggest joker in the current populist pack is the National Rural Employment Guarantee (NREG) Bill, which is to be brought before the next session of Parliament. It could well be a time bomb that does grave damage to India's public finances and development aspirations. On the face of it, the Bill's goals are noble and reasonable (a draft is available on the website of the National Advisory Council (NAC) for the Common Minimum Programme (CMP)). It says that, "Every household in the rural areas of India shall have a right to at least 100 days of guaranteed employment every year for at least one adult member, for doing casual manual labour at the statutory minimum wage...." Moreover, the accompanying explanatory note by Jean Drèze (not apparently a dreaded 'foreign consultant') clarifies that the target population of the employment guarantee is poor rural households, who will 'self-select' for the programme because of the 'conditions of employment'.

Drèze provides an estimate of annual costs. Each person-day would cost Rs. 100, of which Rs. 60 would be wages (approximately, the weighted average of minimum wages for agricultural labour across states) and Rs. 40 for materials and administration. For 100 days this would mean Rs. 10,000 per poor rural household. Since there are approximately four crore rural households below the poverty line (BPL), the total annual cost of the guarantee would come to Rs. 40,000 crore. That would be a hefty 1.3 per cent of current GDP, but allowing for a 4-year phasing in, it could start at 0.5 per cent of GDP and climb to one per cent by 2008/09. In the NAC/Drèze scheme, the wage component of the NREG would be borne by the central government and the material component equally shared by the centre and states. Thus, states would bear only 20 per cent of the costs and also the liability to provide unemployment allowance (at a minimum of one-third of the prevailing minimum wage) in case the administration fails to provide the necessary employment.

In each state, the programme would be administered by the district administrations together with *gram panchayats*, who will issue the necessary 'job cards' to applicants who fulfil the eligibility conditions of rural residence, adulthood and willingness to do casual manual labour at the state's minimum wage for agricultural labour. (Note that being a member of a BPL household is not an eligibility condition).

The crucial weakness of the scheme (and the costing estimates summarised above) is the presumption that only members of poor rural households will 'self-select' themselves as applicants for the NREG. There are at least two reasons to seriously doubt this fundamental assumption. First, in many states people work at below the statutory minimum wage, which is rarely enforced under the ground realities of rural employment. So, many non-poor agricultural workers could switch from existing agricultural employment to the NREG.

Second, and more importantly, the scope for fake muster rolls and doctored job cards is enormous. With the job card as the main document for recording work done and claiming wage payment, it is easy to see that this piece of paper will become the key qualification for wage payment under the scheme, not any actual work done on a project site. In most of rural India, the realities of governance/administration may not distinguish between real and fake claims for work done under the NREG. In effect, the job card could quickly approximate a check for Rs. 6,000 (Rs. 60/day for 100 days) per year, with some discounts for appropriate 'document processing'. If this is the reality, then almost every rural household will aspire to possess at least one job card. Drèze's presumption of 'self-selection' by the rural poor could prove comprehensively wrong as could his estimates of the NREG's annual costs. As Sunil Jain (*Business Standard*, October 25, 2004) has pointed out, the more relevant number for rural households eligible for the scheme then becomes 15 crore, not the 4 crore assumed by NAC/Drèze. And the associated fiscal bill rises towards a mind-boggling Rs. 150,000 crore per year or about 5 per cent of GDP! (If one contemplates the possibility—not wholly remote—of two job cards per rural household, these numbers double!).

That would certainly destroy India's public finances and much else besides. Amongst other casualties would be growth in output and employment, including rural employment (of a real sort, not the likely fictions stimulated by the NREG), any semblance of moderate inflation and whatever limited capacity for development still possessed by the Indian state. The costs of such possible breakdown would be most devastating for the rural poor, precisely the group that the NREG is aimed at helping! But then, the costs of well-intentioned but ill-conceived populist policies are often borne by the poorest in a society.

Confronted by such gloomy prospects, what should we do? The most logical and first best option would be to do nothing, except perhaps focus on improving existing programmes of food for work and rural employment generation. Alas, politics rules over logic. Given the commitments made by the UPA government, some version of the NREG appears inevitable. What can be done to contain the damage and improve the benefits from the programme? The biggest incentive for leakage and abuse arises from the wide gap between the predominantly central funding of the scheme and the predominantly state/local responsibility for its administration. One way of restricting an open-ended (and possibly ruinous) central liability is to cap it on a reasonable basis, such as by limiting central funding for the programme in each state to a product of its estimated number of rural poor households, its minimum wage for agricultural labour, 100 (days) and 0.8 (the centre's share in total costs). Any costs greater than this would be borne by the respective state, thereby providing a strong incentive to states to minimise leakage and abuse of the scheme. This would be consistent with the NAC/Drèze proposals.

Second, and for the same reason, the legal guarantee for the scheme should be given by the respective states, including bearing the responsibility for bearing the unemployment allowance (in case a state fails to provide employment to eligible applicants), as proposed by NAC/Drèze. Third, to ensure states' commitment to the programme, it is important to maintain their share in the costs at the minimum of 20 per cent (corresponding to half the costs of materials and administration) proposed by NAC/Drèze. Fourth, the scheme should be implemented in a phased manner over four or five years, allowing for modification from lessons learned.

None of this will guarantee the success of the programme. Nothing can. But without such reasonable checks there is a high probability of the ironic (and tragic) outcome that the Finance Minister who steered the nation out of an economic crisis in the early nineties might preside, as Prime Minister, over the genesis of the next fiscal crisis.

4

Reviving industrial employment

Perhaps the greatest success of China's extraordinary economic resurgence has been the transformation of a poor, largely rural economy into a semi-industrialised, middle income country with 40 per cent of its GDP coming from manufacturing, over a 100 million factory jobs and over $ 500 billion of manufactured exports. In contrast, India's manufacturing sector has stagnated at around 16 per cent of GDP, employs only about 6 million workers in the organised sector (and perhaps, another 50 million in small, unorganised units with less than 10 workers) and exports around $ 60 billion of goods. Quite clearly, the growth of manufacturing output and employment has been much weaker in India than in China. In particular, India's manufacturing sector has failed to provide a large number of good 'blue collar' job opportunities as the labour force grew and the share of agriculture in GDP fell from over 50 per cent (*circa* 1950) to just over 20 per cent, at present. As a result, nearly 60 per cent of India's 400 million strong labour force remains 'stuck' in low-productivity agriculture, severely compounding the problems of poverty and regional disparities.

Most analysts point to four major policy failures in past decades as the principal culprits for industrial underperformance in India. First, the inward-looking foreign trade policies of an overvalued exchange rate, tight import controls and very high tariffs greatly discouraged Indian manufacturers from seeking export markets at a time (1960 onwards) when world trade was booming and the 'East Asian tiger economies' developed through rapid growth of labour-intensive manufactures. Second, the policy of small-scale industry (SSI) reservations, initiated in 1967 and greatly expanded in 1980, shut out medium and large-scale Indian firms from precisely those labour-intensive products (garments, shoes, toys, sporting goods, etc.) in which the East Asian tigers made their early billions from exporting. Third, there was the chronically bad state of infrastructure, provided by government monopoly agencies like State Electricity Boards, PWD road makers and the telecom department. Last, but by no means least, was the heritage of restrictive labour laws, especially the insertion of chapter V(B) into the Industrial Disputes Act, during the Emergency year, 1976, and its subsequent tightening in 1982. These laws prevented retrenchment and closure of industrial enterprises by requiring (rarely given) government permission. Such inflexibility in lay offs of employees hugely discouraged fresh employment (or new investment) in units with more than 100 workers.

There has been some progress in the last 15 years. Trade and exchange rate policies have undergone major reform: the exchange rate is realistic and market-responsive, most import tariffs have been phased down to 15 per cent and the hideous edifice of import licensing controls has been dismantled. As a result, exports have done well, especially in the mid-nineties and in the last five years. More recently, the commodity coverage of SSI reservations has been reduced, with selective freeing up of goods with significant export potential. Infrastructure remains bad, with the conspicuous exception of telecom, where serious reforms have triggered a big boom in connectivity, empowering millions of individuals and businesses. The heritage of anti-employment labour laws remains unreformed, despite the forthright recommendations of Planning Commission Task Forces and the Second National Commission on Labour. The latter also recommended the repeal of the offending chapter V(B) of the Industrial Disputes Act.

The combination of anti-employment incentives embedded in labour laws and the rigours of a more competitive economy appears to have actually led to a decline in the number of organised sector manufacturing jobs from a peak of 6.9 million in 1997 to 6 million in 2003 (*Economic Survey 2004/05*). Just 6 million. Only 1.5 per cent of India's labour force is employed in organised manufacturing units! This is at a time when the Planning Commission estimates the 'annual increment' in the labour force to be nearly 3 per cent or almost 12 million job-seekers. The situation is not just grim; it's desperate. Yet, the apologists for the *status quo* trot out their routine arguments. Let's consider them:

Argument 1: Why get exercised about labour laws when they apply to less than 5 per cent of the labour force (excluding government employees)? It's 'hire and fire' for the remaining 90 plus per cent.

Counter: The low share of the organised sector in total employment is precisely the problem. We want the proportion of workforce with good jobs to be much higher. Indeed, if chapter V(B) had not been introduced in 1976, the share of the organised sector in total employment might have been 15-20 per cent by now. Restrictive labour laws protect a tiny minority, while encouraging the 'casualisation' of the vast majority of India's workers.

Argument 2: Don't take these labour laws too seriously. Indian businessmen know how to work around them. Can't you see that many have downsized their workforces despite the laws?

Counter: Yes, but the costs of such downsizing (legal and illegal) to firms have been very large, sometimes driving them to insolvency. This has driven home to all businesses, the disadvantages of having sizable number of workers on their books. Better to invest in capital-intensive products or find ways of 'casualising' the required workforce. Either way, the net result is many fewer good organised sector jobs.

Argument 3 : Don't worry about labour laws for industrial labour. India's future is in modern services like IT and BPO.

Counter: The rise of the IT/ITES sector is wonderful. But please remember that direct employment in them is only about a million with perhaps another 1-2 million of indirect employment. Such numbers cannot substitute for strong growth of labour-intensive manufacturing jobs of the kind so successfully created in East Asian economies. Besides, IT jobs are typically for college graduates. Where is the employment opportunity for the many millions more of school leavers? Historically, manufacturing has been the major avenue for low-skill, non-agricultural employment in every country which has successfully matched supply and demand in labour markets in the course of economic development and structural change.

I am afraid, the conclusion is inescapable. If we are serious about encouraging the rapid growth of good, non-agricultural jobs, then we have to reform our hugely dysfunctional labour laws. If we can't muster the political will to do that, then just sit back and watch the much-vaunted demographic dividend turn into a nightmare of unemployment, poverty and social conflict.

C

Reforms: on or off?

5

Why did India reform?

A few weeks ago the Global Development Network of international development scholars held their annual conference (in Delhi) on the theme of "Understanding Reform" (worldwide). Predictably, Manmohan Singh was slated to address a plenary session on India's economic reforms. A few days before the event he withdrew because of political commitments and the conference organisers roped me in to field as substitute. They also asked me to avoid the well-worn story of the 1991 crisis, the ensuing reform programme and its impact on the Indian economy. Instead, they wanted me to address the question of 'why' economic reforms were successfully initiated, implemented and sustained (without serious rollbacks), paying special heed to political, institutional and external factors of the times. Having put some thoughts together for the conference session, I thought I would share them with readers of this paper.

Looking back, it's pretty clear that political ideology (of the markets *versus* state variety) did not play a significant part in sparking the reforms. The general elections of June 1991, were not fought and won under the banner of economic liberalisation. Economic liberalism had never been a serious part of the Congress credo and it wasn't in 1991. That's not to say that politics played no part in the reform story of the early nineties. The fact that the new Congress government (initially a minority one) stayed in power for a full five-year term, 1991-1996, was very important for sustaining the reform thrust and avoiding serious rollbacks. The fact that the Prime Minister and Finance Minister remained unchanged for the full term, assured an important degree of continuity and coherence in economic policies.

If the political ideology of economic liberalism did not launch the ship of Indian reforms, what did? (I can almost hear my fellow columnist Surjit Bhalla muttering "it sure wasn't Helen of Troy!") The conventional wisdom accords prime importance to the external payments crisis of 1991 and the pressures it generated for serious reorientation of the economic policies and paradigms of the previous four decades. By this account, the situation confronting the new Congress government was one of rapidly depleting confidence, plummeting forex reserves (despite a savage squeeze on imports), fleeing non-resident deposits, rising inflation, declining production and a serious likelihood of an unprecedented external payments default by India. In this grim scenario, the freshly mandated Narasimha Rao turned to an experienced and highly respected technocrat, Manmohan Singh, gave him the finance portfolio and, for a while, support and a free hand with economic policy to get the country out of crisis. So, if necessity is the mother of invention, then the external payments crisis was the mother of reforms!

Broadly speaking, this conventional wisdom is correct. But it does not quite answer some nagging questions. Why did the reforms take the form they did, marking such a radical change with past policies? Why did the implementation of the new policies proceed fairly smoothly? What led to their success in quickly generating good economic outcomes? Why were rollbacks rare? To answer these questions we have to marshal some other factors which played a significant role in India's successful reforms.

First, although economic liberalism (plus prudent fiscal management) was not part of contemporary political ideology in India, most elements of the reform agenda had been around in influential sections of India's 'technocracy' for some years. The partial success with the limited liberalisations of import and industrial controls in the mid-1980s, had also enhanced the spread and commitment to these ideas in the technocracy. All this facilitated quick articulation of a coherent reform programme when crisis created the opportunity for change. Incidentally, contrary to some left-wing fiction, the reform programme was very much 'home grown'. The major international financial institutions (IMF, World Bank, ADB) only played a supportive and constructive role of providing emergency balance of payments financing and bolstering external confidence in the Indian economy.

Second, a key institutional feature which facilitated the design and implementation of the reforms of the early 1990s was the close coordination between the Prime Minister's Office, the Finance Ministry, the Reserve Bank of India and the Commerce Ministry. This, in turn, was helped by the Prime Minister's clear and strong mandate, Manmohan Singh's long and distinguished technocratic service (he had earlier served as RBI Governor, Planning Commission head, Economic Affairs Secretary, Chief Economic Adviser) and consequent ability to command respect and cooperation of the civil service, plus his deliberate programme to build a strong and durable team of economic managers in the Finance Ministry and the RBI. Such durability was important for successful implementation of reforms and for maintaining a consistent 'reform message'.

Third, in the spectrum between 'big bang' and 'gradualism' India's initial reforms are best described as 'medium bang'. This (initially) systemic approach was very important for quickly restoring confidence and for triggering early fruits of reform. The systemic or 'medium bang' nature may be gauged from the fact that within a few months, the following steps had been taken: virtual abolition of industrial licensing; rupee devaluation by 20 per cent; the complex import licensing replaced by a system (EXIMSCRIPS) of tradable, import entitlements earned through exports (later replaced by a dual, and then, market-determined exchange rate); phased reduction of customs duties; fiscal deficit cut by 2 per cent of GDP; foreign investment opened up; banking reforms launched; capital market reforms initiated; initial disinvestment of public enterprises announced and major tax reforms outlined. It certainly helped that most of these early reforms could be implemented by government orders and notifications and did not require legislative enactment.

The initial burst of reforms (with emphasis on deregulation and market orientation) was the key to swift revival of 'domestic' confidence (hence, the investment boom of 1993-1996) and 'external' confidence (hence, the quick rise in foreign investment, external remittances and non-resident deposits). Other good things followed swiftly, helped by the nature of the reforms, the economy's underlying resilience, and a buoyant world economy. GDP growth recovered quickly and strongly to average over 6.5 per cent in the first four post-reform years with strong growth in all major sectors, exports surged by 20 per cent annually in 1993-1996, savings and investment were buoyant, forex reserves quickly climbed from about $ 2 billion to $ 20 billion by early 1995, and the external debt situation improved quickly. This swift turnaround in major economic indicators was important for sustaining the reform momentum, winning converts and preventing serious rollbacks. Thus, the 'early harvest' itself became an ingredient of success with the reforms.

Finally, we should not underestimate the personal factor. The external payments crisis of 1991, certainly generated the pressures and created the opportunity for undertaking long-overdue reforms. But the opportunity had to be seized and held. And for that, India's citizens will forever be in debt to the courage, wisdom and vision of Manmohan Singh. He was the right man in the right place at the right time.

6

Reforms, may be but at what speed?

First things first: I would like to join millions of fellow citizens in conveying best wishes to India's new Prime Minister and his Government. This is both heartfelt and selfish, for on his success and that of his Government will hinge the welfare of all of us.

What about economic reforms? India's 'miracle-maker' of the early 1990s is now the Prime Minister. Can we expect reforms to go full steam ahead? Or will the constraints imposed by the Left parties and others throttle progress? What do we mean by reforms anyway? Such issues will engage us in the months ahead—and lots of trees will be felled to feed the printing presses. In an important sense, only time will reveal the answer to the questions of how fast and how seriously will the new Government proceed with economic reforms. But it's too tempting not to indulge in some initial speculations on the subject. And, to anticipate the conclusion, don't let your expectations run ahead of the political realities!

The phrase 'economic reforms' is much abused. Like the elephant in the *Sufi* parable, it means different things to different people. Often, confusing ends with means, 'reforms' are held to connote higher growth, more employment, less poverty, better education, health and safety nets, etc. Everyone favours such goals. The hard questions of policy relate to how we attain them. For our purpose, let's define 'economic reforms' as those changes in economic policy which will hasten the achievement of these goals, especially faster growth of national output and employment.

What are the key policy thrusts that need to be pursued? I would suggest the following seven priorities. First, the current massive level of government dissaving (revenue deficits) has to be reduced so that private savings fund more of productive investment instead of government consumption. Second, the climate for industrial investment (domestic and foreign) has to be improved so that manufacturing recaptures the dynamism of the mid-nineties. Third, we need policies to increase the job content of output growth. Fourth, to get better returns from savings and investment, the banking sector has to become more modern and efficient. Fifth, we urgently need a policy package to revitalise agriculture. Sixth, policies must focus on reversing the neglect of primary education and primary healthcare. Finally, transformation of our very inefficient electric power sector is long overdue. Based on statements by UPA leaders and reports on the Common Minimum Programme, how much forward movement can we expect in each of these areas?

Reduction of revenue deficits will happen only through increase in the tax-GDP ratio and containment of current government expenditures. At the Centre, the 2003 Fiscal Responsibility Act provides a framework and incentives to move in the right direction. The Left parties usually hail revenue increases (though please remember West Bengal's very low tax ratio). It will be up to the Finance Ministry to secure more of the necessary revenue increases through modernising tax administration and less through increases in tax rates (though the latter should not be ruled out of court). The prospects for containing current government expenditures are considerably dimmer, given the early clamour for state-specific expenditure 'packages' and the known difficulties of imposing the necessary hard-budget constraint on ministries and states in a weak, multiparty coalition.

The modest uptick in industrial output and investment in 2003/04 may have some momentum, especially from the buoyancy of agriculture, unless investor sentiment has been weakened by the political uncertainties of the last two months. The possible stimulus from a strong privatisation programme, further dereservation of more SSI sectors and labour reforms is unlikely to transpire, given the UPA's early policy statements. So what will invigorate industrial output and investment?

There is huge consensus that economic growth has to be far more 'jobful', not jobless as in the nineties. But there is far less consensus on reforming the labour laws which have depressed the growth of modern factory employment in India for decades. The NDA government's proposals of early 2001 remained stillborn. And it's hard to see the Left (or even a public-sector oriented Congress) being farsighted enough to champion such reforms. But without such reforms, it is equally hard to envision 'jobful' growth. How then will the burgeoning labour force of the oft-touted 'demographic dividend' be accommodated?

The Prime Minister seems to have already announced that PSU banks will remain in the public sector. From a reform perspective this is clearly a backward step from the NDA Bill of 2000 (since stuck in parliamentary limbo) to reduce government equity in banks to 33 per cent. At the same time, the manifestos promise building a modern financial sector. Looking around at global experience, it's impossible to find a serious country where financial modernisation has occurred in a predominantly public sector banking system. There is the additional serious risk of heightened pressure for directed and behest lending by government-owned banks. We have paid the costs of such misdirected lending before.

Revitalising agriculture will require much greater investments in (and maintenance of) rural infrastructure of irrigation, roads, soil conservation, etc. and reinvigoration of the present systems of agricultural research and extension. While the new Central Government can play a significant role in revamping systems, the main responsibility for strengthening rural infrastructure lies with the States. And their finances are under such stress that it is difficult to see how they will find the money, especially if (as in Andhra Pradesh and Tamil Nadu) hard-won gains of partial cost recovery (for power and other services) are squandered overnight.

The primacy of the States' role holds true also for education and health. As does the pervasive problem of stressed State finances. Still, the Central Government can play an important supporting role through various channels, including strategic centrally-sponsored schemes and dissemination of successful lessons in enhancing accountability of teachers and improvements in curricula and examination systems. It can certainly discharge this role more effectively, if the concerned central ministry is not preoccupied with revision of history books, reducing the autonomy of institutions of higher learning and labouring over schemes to hugely increase subsidies to richer students in management institutes!

Every Indian (outside Lutyens' Delhi!) knows about the disgraceful state of our electric power sector. A significant portion of our GDP comes from the production of generators, inverters, stabilisers and other paraphernalia which are unknown in more 'normal' countries! The NDA government's recent new Electricity Act has wrought a major improvement in the policy framework for electricity generation and distribution. Optimists say that it will usher in a new era for this sector. I hope so. But I also hope that the new government will undertake the follow through, necessary to realise this new potential. As for states which revert to dispensing free power, I hope that neither the Central Government nor the Finance Commission will underwrite their profligacy.

So what does the above review of seven policy thrusts necessary to accelerate growth of output and employment augur for the enterprise of economic reforms? Not, I fear, a resounding clarion call for resurgent reforms. Interestingly, the new government seems to have much more enthusiasm for forging ahead in areas (such as agriculture, education and health) which are mainly in the domain of the states. Conversely, it shows a decidely more lukewarm approach to fiscal consolidation, industrial climate, privatisation, banking and labour reforms, areas where the policy levers are more in the Centre's ambit. It does seem that the spirit of the CMP (or is it LCD?) might damp those of the 'Good Doctor'.

7

Bad ideas *versus* good men

The UPA has governed for a month. During this period, Gresham's law ("bad money drives out good money") seems to have held sway in the realm of economic ideas. The Common Minimum Programme (CMP) has been a fertile breeding ground for many bad ideas. Subsequent pronouncements by ministers (or reports of their forthcoming initiatives) have also contributed their fair share. Over the same period, the government's top economic management team has taken shape, with Manmohan Singh as prime minister, P. Chidambaram as finance minister and (most recently) Montek Ahluwalia as deputy chairman, Planning Commission. It would be difficult, perhaps impossible, to conceive a stronger economic top team at cabinet level. Yet their exceptionally high calibre makes for intriguing contrast with the poor quality of economic ideas swirling around in the CMP and ministerial pronouncements. Such tension between bad ideas and good economic managers cannot persist indefinitely. Economic governance over the next few months should be a fascinating battle between good men and bad ideas, a battle which will yield winners and losers.

Since the quality of the top team is hardly at issue, this piece will dwell on some of the bad economic ideas ambient in current economic policy documents and pronouncements. Let's start with the CMP.

Item: a National Employment Guarantee Act to guarantee 100 days employment per year at minimum wages for at least one able bodied person in each rural household. Several analysts have already noted the massive fiscal costs of this proposal and the dubious value of assets that might be created. The organisational challenge is also daunting. Then there is the fundamental issue of long-term sustainability of such 'make work' programmes.

Item: 'Fullest implementation' of minimum wage laws for farm labour. It's hard to think of a more fearsome anti-poor, anti-employment measure than this innocuous sounding commitment. Let's hope it's not meant seriously or, alternatively, 'fullest implementation' connotes the *status quo*.

Item: Raise public spending on education to at least 6 per cent of GDP. Aside from the obvious problem of resources, this promise (and the similar one on health) totally misses the real problems of ineffective service delivery and absence of accountability in the bulk of our public social sector service systems.

Item: Government will be "sensitive to the issue of affirmative action, including reservations, in the private sector." If sensitivity leads to enactment of reservations in private sector employment, they will become huge disincentives against any fresh employment and will, at one stroke, grievously undermine the international competitiveness of Indian firms. And the costs in terms of social conflict could be awesome.

Item: 'generally' profit-making, public sector companies will not be privatised. That pretty much terminates existing policies for disinvestment/privatisation. The capital market has certainly taken that view and hugely reduced stock valuations of PSUs. Corridor gossip confirms serious inactivity in the Department of Disinvestment. As for loss-making enterprises, the chances of successful sales by government are next to nil. Who will have the courage to set reserve prices low enough to allow successful transactions?

Item: Go slow on reform of labour laws. These laws have probably been the single most potent cause of stagnating employment in organised industry. Going slow with their reform means going slow with industrial job creation.

Perhaps, the CMP is not meant to be taken seriously? So why worry about the bad ideas and policy suggestions that litter the document? So runs the siren song of some optimistic commentators. To them I would say, beware! A massive National Advisory Council to oversee implementation of the CMP is apparently being established and will be headed by Congress president, Sonia Gandhi. Besides, most of the policies noted above have been repeated in the President's address to Parliament making them tantamount to government policy.

The CMP has not been the sole source of bad economic ideas in the past month. There have been others. Take the case of the steel price regulatory authority mooted by the Minister for Steel. The proposal is redolent with all the bad old ways of the 'licence-permit *raj*'. Lest you treat it lightly, be warned that the machinery of the Iron and Steel Comptroller and the Joint Plant Committee still exist and can be swiftly activated. Most disquieting is the fact that there has not been (to the best of my knowledge) any contrary reassurance from either the Prime Minister or the Finance Minister. Contrast this inaction with the swift bringing to heel of the External Affairs Minister when he seemed to stray a bit from the 'no Indian troops in Iraq' doctrine while holding a joint press conference with Colin Powell in Washington, recently.

Another bad old idea that appears to have been resurrected is that of having a national investment commission or investment promotion board, tasked with promoting investment (mainly, domestic) in the country. Such a body is likely to be dysfunctional at best and obstructive at worst. We already have several departments of industry and industrial development whose prime task should be to promote healthy industrial growth and investment. We don't need new administrative organs to promote investment. We need better economic policies and better infrastructure. If we have those, more investment will happen. If we don't, no amount of administrative tinkering will do the job. Yes, at the level of states, promotional bodies can speed up allotment of land, water and electricity connections and various approvals.

Most states already have such organs; they are dormant in some states and effective in others.

A third dubious (and very, very old) idea doing the rounds, is that of sharply expanding rural credit. This one has been thought of quite frequently, approximately once a year at budget time! The underlying problems are deep-seated and include a floundering system of cooperative credit institutions, bankrupt regional rural banks and serious weaknesses in the real agricultural economy. Loading this creaking system with politically-driven increases in credit is simply paving the way for more bad loans and more fiscal bailouts of credit institutions in future. Given the past history of similar compulsions, a good hard look at NABARD's balance sheet may be more urgent than exhorting that apex organ to pump up rural credit.

As you can see, there's no lack of bad economic ideas. Indeed, it's hard to keep them from bubbling over (it reminds me of a pithy comment on our politics by a wise old friend when he said "in Indian politics it's impossible to keep a bad man down"! The current controversy about 'tainted ministers' vindicates his quip). Seven decades ago, John Maynard Keynes, the father of macroeconomics, warned against the pernicious influence of bad old ideas on current economic policy. Today, in India, we look to a few good men in the top economic management team to hold back the tide of bad ideas and advance real economic reforms. We should wish them luck from the bottom of our hearts.

8

Bad ideas are winning

Six months ago (*Business Standard,* June 22, 2004) I noted the "intriguing contrast" between the 'exceptionally high calibre' of this government's top economic management team (Manmohan Singh, P. Chidambaram and Montek Ahluwalia) and the "poor quality of economic ideas swirling around in the Common Minimum Programme and ministerial pronouncements." I went on to predict that, "Such tension between bad ideas and good economic managers cannot persist indefinitely. Economic governance over the next few months should be a fascinating battle between good men and bad ideas, a battle which will yield winners and losers." Half a year later, with 2004 coming to a close, it's time for an initial stocktaking. With profound sadness I have to record that 'bad ideas' seem to be prevailing over 'good men'. Let me substantiate. And let me organise the dispiriting evidence under some policy categories.

Employment creation

Most economists agree that our complex and inflexible labour laws are probably the single most important cause of stagnant employment in the organised segment of the economy, especially industry. The CMP dimmed hopes of progress in this area. And sure enough, there has been none. Correspondingly, the prospects for rapid growth of good jobs in modern factory employment remain dim.

Instead, the government has opted to fulfil the CMP promise of an Employment Guarantee Act and has tabled a bill in Parliament last fortnight. I will not repeat my profound concerns about its onerous fiscal consequences (*Business Standard*, November 30, 2004). Others have also emphasised the large scope for corruption and 'leakages' and the costs of diverting scarce resources from social and economic infrastructure. Many analysts agree that the new act will, over time, develop into a horribly expensive gravy train for political patronage with little durable 'benefit' for the poor. Political expediency will dictate the expansion of the 'benefits' of the scheme, quite independent of its efficacy in serving the avowed objectives.

Restructuring the public sector

Public enterprises continue to dominate large chunks of the Indian economy, especially energy, banking, insurance and transportation. This is despite almost a decade of ministerial pronouncements to the effect that, "the business of government is not business." As envisaged in the CMP, the privatisation process is pretty dead in the water. Predictably, talk of selling loss-making enterprises remains just that, talk. Even disinvestment, in the sense of selling minority shareholding to the public, is taking the slow train.

Indeed, a new Board for Reconstruction of Public Sector Enterprises has just replaced the old Disinvestment Commission. Apparently, its focus will be on reviving PSEs. No matter that many years and many thousands of crores of wasted government money have demonstrated the utter futility of pursuing this objective. Ask any of the last five Union expenditure secretaries. What's more, the new Board has been established even before the old BIFR has gracefully left the stage, prompting this newspaper to editorially coin (December 23, 2004) "a new Parkinson's Law which stipulates that sick public sector companies will not only not die but bodies to revive them will proliferate!"

Infrastructure

The follow through on the Electricity Act (2003) remains slow. Indeed, there is some question as to whether the 'review' threatened in the CMP is really behind us or not. Railway finances, organisations and operations are still as immune to reform as ever, notwithstanding the metronomic regularity of major accidents. National highway development continues as a bright spot, even as state and rural roads languish for lack of funds and maintenance. The decade old plans to privatise the national airlines seem to have been shelved, while the good intentions to induct the private sector in metro airport development, remain vulnerable to political hurdles, regulatory uncertainties and state government caprices. Telecom is forging ahead despite regulatory favouritism but urban infrastructure development continues to be mired in dismal municipal finances and governance. In energy, coal development is stalled by a potent brew of ideology and *mafia* politics, while oil and gas remain hostage to administered prices, political whims and oligopolistic behemoths, public and private. Not much is being done to forestall the water wars in our future.

The Planning Commission has been struggling manfully with these key infrastructure issues, although it did get distracted temporarily by a weird and unworkable scheme to use forex for infrastructure finance. In short, the policy thrusts to address the country's immense infrastructure needs are still incremental and inadequate.

Financial sector

Whatever happened to the brave new world of financial sector reforms? Well, the NDA government in its final year rolled back earlier progress by boosting 'directed credit', proliferating interest rates and pursuing pointless mergers of government-controlled financial intermediaries. The UPA government appears distressingly comfortable with these retrograde tendencies. Government ownership of PSU banks has been firmly reiterated. A confusing flirtation continues with the issue of higher foreign ownership in private banks. What is patently lacking is a long-term vision for the banking sector. If the dominant elements of the implicit game plan are government control, heavy directed credit and significant interest rate controls, then the campaign slogans about a modern financial sector should be quietly buried.

The private insurance sector is maturing steadily. Growth would be faster if the last budget's commitment to raise the equity cap on foreign ownership through amendment of law had not run into implacable opposition from the Left and a tetchy BJP. The Left is also successfully blocking the lifting of the cap on foreign shareholding in telecom and foreign participation in the retail sector. The government's weakness in this area is also shown by its apparent flip-flop on the dilution of Press Note 18, which is currently tilted in favour of the domestic partner in foreign collaborations.

Tax reforms

The last budget did not help the cause of tax reform. A bad tax on stock transactions was launched somewhat clumsily. Taxation of long-term equity capital gains was abolished, creating a distinctly uncomfortable situation (for a poor country) in which owners of (equity) capital are neither taxed on dividend earnings nor on capital gains, while all forms of labour income are taxable. If the Left was less preoccupied with outdated sloganeering and a little more thoughtful, it might have raised cogent objections to such proposals.

While the date for inducting state VATs has been reset for April 1, 2005, the reports about the likely design are quite disconcerting. In particular, a wide dispersion of rates and the slotting of a very large number of commodities at the concessional four per cent rate do not augur at all well for this VAT experiment. And whatever happened to the Kelkar ideas for a national goods and services tax? The government has not encouraged any serious debate on them.

Well, that's quite a lot of bad ideas for just six months. There isn't much of a clarion call for economic reform in any of the above. Where are the good men in all this? Overwhelmed, under siege or complicit? Perhaps a bit of all three? Is there no silver lining? Well may be there is. It's in the resilience of the Indian economy and the dynamism of its people. As we look forward to a new year, let us hope that this resilience and dynamism reinvigorates the 'good men' to fight the good fight and subdue the 'bad ideas'...and perhaps even implement some good ones!

9

Populism rides again

As 2005 draws to a close, it's tempting to take stock of the broad themes which seem to have emerged in economic policies and developments over the past year. I can't help feeling that the dominant theme has been one of resurgent populism. What do I mean by populism? I am referring to economic and social policies which are popular (especially, to politicians) in the short-run but which are fundamentally ill-conceived and inimical to the long-term economic and social progress of the country. Of course, all democratic governments indulge in populism; it is an inevitable part of competitive democratic politics. But when populism becomes the *lietmotif* of a government's policies, watch out for its massive economic and social costs in the coming years.

The arch exponent of populism was Indira Gandhi (her 1966-1977 government), with her "garibi hatao" slogan, kitchen socialism and penchant for legislating government control over economic activities and agents. Just recall some of her populist initiatives, which may have won her votes then but lingered on to undermine India's economic performance for decades. There was: the nationalisations of banks (1969) and insurance (1970), whose legacies still dominate and hobble our financial sector; the introduction of small-scale industry reservations (1967), which was to throttle our comparative advantage for exporting labour-intensive manufactures for over three decades; the Monopolies and Restrictive Trade Practices Act (1969), which curbed expansion of large firms; the draconian Foreign Exchange Regulation Act

(FERA, 1973), which deified the false god of foreign exchange scarcity, spawned a stifling (and corrupt) edifice of forex and import controls and justified a myriad sins of economic policy; the hiking of direct tax rates to stratospheric levels, which gave a huge fillip to evasion and the black economy; the severe tightening of the Industrial Disputes Act (1976), which made it virtually impossible to retrench industrial workers and thus, choked the incentives for fresh employment to this day.

All these actions were, of course, justified (perhaps, even motivated) by noble sentiments such as expanding banking services to rural areas, curbing industrial monopolies, nurturing small industries, husbanding scarce foreign exchange, deploying taxation for equitable redistribution and protecting workers' rights. But their actual consequences for economic development were quite devastating. The period 1967-1980 (yes, the Janata government was also populist) witnessed painfully slow growth of per capita GDP at barely 1.5 per cent and productivity growth of less than one per cent a year, with the national poverty ratio staying stubbornly above 50 per cent. Poverty was anything but "hataoed"! Indeed, the partial reforms of Rajiv Gandhi and the more far-reaching reforms of the 1990s can be largely construed as efforts to roll back the misguided economic initiatives of Indira Gandhi.

Indira Gandhi had no monopoly over Indian economic populism. The V.P. Singh government gave the country huge write-offs of rural credits and the massive, Mandalite expansion of reservations in public sector jobs and educational facilities, thereby seriously weakening meritocratic principles in the functioning of education and administration. The United Front government's decisions on the Fifth Pay Commission report in 1997, bloated government salary and pension bills and undermined severely the states' capacities for providing effective public services in social and economic arenas.

In the 21 years after Indira Gandhi, there have been two periods when populism, while not absent, has taken a backseat in the framing of economic policies: the five years of Rao-Singh economic reforms during 1991-1996 and the period of NDA government, 1998-2004. Judging by the events of the past year or so, the Gandhi

(Sonia)-Singh led UPA coalition seems to have brought populism back to the driver's seat of economic policymaking. Consider the following examples. The new Rural Employment Guarantee Act could prove horribly expensive and provide a gravy train of political patronage with little meaningful impact on rural employment and poverty. The Delhi Congress government's retreats on electricity and water reform in the face of well-heeled, populist pressure reduces hopes for urban infrastructure reform, as does the recent Union Cabinet's nod for dilution of the 2003, Electricity Act. The demonstrated reluctance to pass on international oil price increases to domestic users and the preference for burdening our oil companies with large subsidy bills does not augur well for sensible energy policy. The recent constitutional amendment to enable reservations in private, unaided educational institutions is fraught with plenty of long-term, efficiency-reducing consequences. As if such populist measures were not enough, there is an ill-conceived bill for social insurance of informal sector workers lurking in the wings.

This populist resurgence has occurred against the background of stalled reforms in agriculture, labour laws, electric power, banking, privatisation, pensions and employee provident funds. It raises the intriguing question: if reforms are stalled and populist policies are riding high, how come the economy is performing so well, turning in the third successive year of 7 per cent (or higher) growth, with inflation moderate and external finances reasonably robust? There could be several answers. First, the growth may not be quite as strong as government data indicate. For some time, I have been voicing the heretical suspicion that the sustained strong growth of the services sector (accounting for more than half of GDP and 70 per cent of all economic growth after 1997) at 8 per cent plus since 1997, may reflect statistical infirmities more than reality. Such doubts are not helped by the CSO's reluctance to publish an updated "Sources and Methods" for many years. Second, the last couple of years have clearly seen an upswing in the industrial cycle, buoyed by an unexpectedly robust international economic environment and a more open Indian economy. Neither the industrial upswing nor the global economic buoyancy is guaranteed to last. Third, and perhaps most important, the economic costs of populism typically balloon over time. Which is why populist policies are difficult to resist in the short-run cycle of competitive (and myopic) democratic politics. But, as history shows, their long-run consequences can be seriously negative.

The only effective remedy against the obvious political temptations of populism, lies with the country's leadership and their motivation, courage and ability to protect long-term national interests from short-term political opportunism. Such leadership was provided by Rao-Singh in 1991-1996 and Vajpayee-Advani-Sinha in 1998-2004. As the new year dawns, we can only hope that Sonia Gandhi and Manmohan Singh can rise to the challenge of keeping populism at bay in 2006. The record of 2005 is not promising.

10

Economic policy: mid-term report

In a few weeks the UPA government will reach the mid-point of its five year term. It's an opportune moment to assess the government's economic policy record (my focus is on 'policy' rather than outcomes, since the latter typically come with a lag and are also influenced by other factors such as global economic conditions). I have chosen 10 key policy dimensions and ascribed (subjectively) marks out of a maximum of 10 for each, with the proviso of giving a minimum of 2 marks as sort of 'grace' marks or to cover some good policies I may have overlooked. Broadly speaking, the first 5 policy dimensions are 'macro' and the latter 5 'sectoral'. The marks are in the Table 10.1 but let me comment briefly on each assessment.

Fiscal policy

There are really three key aspects here: the overall fiscal balance/ deficit, taxation and expenditure policies. The Centre's gross fiscal deficit has indeed improved from 4.5 per cent of GDP in 2003/04 (pre-UPA) to 4.1 per cent in 2005/06. But the primary (non-interest) deficit has actually widened over this period from marginally negative to plus 0.5 per cent of GDP, which is quite worrying now that we are clearly on the upswing of the interest rate cycle. Furthermore, FRBM targets have already been twice 'paused' or postponed formally by the UPA government. Even the fiscal deficit improvement is illusory on correct accounting, after factoring in the 'oil bonds' issued by government. Tax policies have been a mixed bag, with some good measures (such as peak customs tariff reductions and integration of service taxes in the Modvat framework) and some bad (such as the FBT, the cash withdrawal tax and the generous exemptions for SEZs). Expenditure initiatives have mainly accommodated the government's populist proclivities; there has been no serious restructuring to support stronger economic development in future. Hence, '4' would seem to be appropriate.

Money/Banking

In contrast, monetary policy has adroitly balanced the triple objectives of moderating inflation, nurturing growth and encouraging orderly foreign exchange markets. The RBI has done well despite the occasional, ill-timed *diktat* from the finance ministry (such as the recent one to public sector banks on interest rates). Banking is another story, with no progress in dilution of government ownership or in effective enhancement of bank autonomy. Treasury profits (from the interest rate downswing) and buoyant economic conditions have masked underlying weaknesses (in technology, personnel, 'commercial culture' and managerial autonomy) of many public sector banks. It's going to be tougher in future, especially with the government's policy relapse into directed lending and interest rate controls. Overall policy coordination between North Block (which has primary responsibility) and the RBI has been manifestly weak at times. Taken as a package, '5' would seem reasonable.

Exchange rate/external payments

Against a background of continuing strong capital inflows (which have augmented forex reserves by about $ 50 billion since UPA took charge) and rising oil prices, RBI (presumably with government support) has prevented undue real appreciation of the rupee, nurtured two-way variation in the exchange rate, and moderated excess volatility. This has been no mean feat, especially in view of the concomitant challenge to 'sterilise' the monetary consequences of reserve accretion. The approach to payments liberalisation has been cautiously positive, rightly so despite what some 'market fundamentalist' academics may advocate. The successful management of the exchange rate has been a key determinant of dynamic exports (goods and services) and steadily rising inward remittances. Hence, my award of '8' marks here.

Employment policies

With India's burgeoning labour force (over 400 million already and expected to rise above 650 million by 2020) the importance of jobful growth is obvious...and critical. Unfortunately, our present labour laws discourage employment expansion and encourage casualisation, while 'protecting' the seven per cent of workers in the organised sector (including government). The UPA government, in thrall to this minority of privileged workers, has undertaken no reform of labour laws. The new rural employment guarantee programme is only a 'make work' scheme (not real job creation), which suffers from serious design flaws. It's better suited for conferring political patronage (and corruption) than job creation. Hence, the grace mark of '2' in this crucial area.

Public sector reform

Well, there hasn't been any to speak of, even though it has become much more urgent with the stuttering halt of the disinvestment/privatisation programme. Despite lots of promises and committees on administrative reform, actual progress is absent. Another '2' I fear.

Trade and industry

There has been modest (but welcome) progress on the well-established paths of reducing peak customs duties and pruning the list of items reserved for small-scale industry. The fondness for regional trade pacts is a global disease (the UPA has also succumbed), which cannot really substitute for multilateral trade liberalisation. The UPA's showpiece industrial initiative is the SEZ scheme. Will it really boost additional investment (as opposed to diversion) and at what cost in tax revenues and land scams? The scope for the latter two seems ominously large. A '5' would be generous.

Agriculture

This crucially important sector has grown at less than a measly two per cent since 1996/97. The UPA has not produced any significant policy solutions for the sector's well-known problems. Its draft 11th Plan Approach Paper describes the 'collapse' and disarray in agricultural extension, cooperative credit and water management systems. The sclerotic preoccupation with wheat and rice continues to hurt the development of coarse grains, pulses and non-food agriculture. A hugely disappointing '2'.

Human resource development

The most prominent UPA policy initiative, reservation for OBCs in higher education, is also the worst. Based on lots of political opportunism and little serious analysis, it could seriously damage the already strained higher education system without improving social equity. Meanwhile, throwing more money at a crumbling and unresponsive public school system is solving few problems. Another very disappointing '2'.

Energy policy

If pampered Delhi's summer outages and the stubbornly high SEB deficits are yardsticks, the UPA has done little to solve the country's endemic power shortages. The government's response to higher oil prices has been equally weak and subsidy-prone. Coal remains nationalised and subject to depredations of political *mafias*. The genuinely bold nuclear deal offers a silver lining, but for the long-run. A '3' at best.

Other infrastructure

The breakthrough on private airport development is truly commendable. Progress on national highway development and better railway performance are also welcome. But state roads and urban infrastructure (especially water and sanitation) remain deplorable, despite some initiatives. A '5' perhaps.

Totting up, that yields a 'barely passing' 21 (out of 50) for 'macro' policies, a shameful 17 (out of 50) for 'sectoral' policies and a flunking 38 per cent overall.

If policy is this bad, how come the economy is growing at 8 per cent? For clues to this puzzle, see chap. 13.

Table 10.1

Economic policy: mid-term report card

Policy area	*Marks* (out of 10)
Macro	
1. Fiscal	4
2. Money/banking	5
3. Exchange rate/external payments	8
4. Employment	2
5. Public sector reform	2
(Sub-total) (21)	
Sectoral	
6. Trade and industry	5
7. Agriculture	2
8. Human resource development	2
9. Energy	3
10. Other infrastructure	5
(Sub-total) (17)	
Total	**38**

D

Economic growth

11

What's happening in services?

The hype about India's newfound services prowess continues unabated. You could be forgiven for thinking that every second member of the country's labour force is either scaling new infotech frontiers in Bangalore or learning Texan accents in a call centre in Noida or Gurgaon. Normally, sober analysts are painting visions of a global future, where China supplies all the world's demand for goods while India meets global needs for services.

There is, of course, a germ of truth in all this, mixed in with large dollops of hyperbole, exaggeration and unrealistic hopes. To restore a modicum of realism and perspective on the matter, let's begin with a few numbers. Table 11.1 shows the evolving structure of India's services sector and the varying growth rates of individual subsectors. By 2000/01, services activities accounted for nearly half of India's economy. But notice that the vaunted subsectors of IT and BPO are nowhere in sight. Actually, they are tucked away under 'business services', which accounted for just 1.1 per cent of GDP in 2000/01. That's about the same as 'personal services', which hardly anybody mentions. What's more, business services measure up to only a fifth of 'community services', even less of 'banking' and 'public administration; defence', and less than a tenth of distributive 'trade'. Indeed, the 'increment' in the share of the trade sector in the nineties is substantially greater than the entire business services sector in 2000/01!

With services accounting for around half of GDP in India and many developing countries and up to 70 per cent of GDP in some industrialised economies, one would have expected far greater economic analysis of this predominant chunk of real world economies. Alas, the economists tribe have preferred to plough the familiar fields of industry, agriculture, public finance, trade in goods, etc. The doctoral dissertations on productivity are usually about manufacturing or agriculture. There is lots of debate on industrial recessions…when did you last read about services recession? Such biased focus is really quite astonishing. All the more reason to rejoice when a serious paper comes along on services. J. Gordon and P. Gupta (henceforth, GG) presented their thought-provoking paper, "Understanding India's Services Revolution" at an IMF-NCAER seminar last month. For the benefit of the readers, let me summarise some of the broad facts and themes from their research.

First, there had been a marked acceleration in services sector growth in the eighties and nineties, especially in the latter. Thus, while the share of services in India's GDP increased by 21 per cent points in the 50 years between 1950 and 2000, nearly 40 per cent of that increase was concentrated in the nineties decade. Second, while almost all service sectors participated in this boom, growth was fastest in communications, financial services, hotels/restaurants, community services, trade and business services. These segments fully account for the acceleration in services growth displayed by the CSO data in the nineties. Third, while up to 1990, India was neatly on the cross-country fitted line-plotting services share against per capita income, the nineties' acceleration took her services share a good five per cent points above the cross-country norm. Fourth, India's services boom was relatively 'jobless': the rise in services share in GDP was not accompanied by any increase in the sector's share of national employment. In a cross-country 'fit' of services share in employment against the share in GDP, India is a clear outlier, well below the fitted line.

The GG paper is rich in analysis, including an interesting exploration of factors that may have fuelled the recent services boom in India. But let me also voice a couple of reservations. In their historical analysis of the data, GG ignore an 'outlier' characteristic I have pointed to on a number of occasions. By this I refer to the curious fact that while the growth of services in India has been very close to the trajectory of industrial growth from 1950, all the way up to 1996/97, there is a marked divergence in the trajectories in the Ninth Plan period, 1997-2002 when services grew at 8 per cent and industry at only 4.5 per cent. Such anomalous trends are also not seen in other developing countries and call for some explanation. Above all, it raises the issue of sustainability of strong services growth in the absence of a sustained industrial recovery.

Secondly, GG conduct their analysis of the CSO data on services without assessing their quality. It's a well-known fact that the estimates of value added in services sectors in India (and most developing countries) are based on much weaker data than corresponding estimates for the main commodity producing sectors of industry and agriculture. Let me convey a flavour of this by quoting from a CSO publication describing how gross value added (GVA) in the subsector 'ownership of dwellings'(as an example) is estimated: "The GVA for the ownership of dwellings is equivalent to the gross rental of the residential census houses less the cost of repairs and maintenance. The number of 1991 census residential houses in urban and rural areas are projected to get the estimates for...1993-94 by applying the average compound growth rates between 1981 and 1991 residential houses..." This is combined with "rent per household obtained from results of the Household Consumption Expenditure Survey 1993-94 (50th Round NSS)...to estimate gross rental separately for rural and urban areas. Cost of repair and maintenance...have been subtracted from gross rental to obtain estimates of GVA for rural and urban areas in the base year (1993-94). For subsequent years (after 1993-94) the constant price estimates have been obtained by multiplying the rent per household with projected residential census houses (...projected by applying the average compound growth rate between 1981 and 1991)."

Thus for, say, 1998/99 estimates of GVA in this sector, the rental information comes from the 1993/94 survey and the housing stock data relies on the growth of houses between 1981 and 1991. No data for the actual year 1998/99 is used! Similar methods are deployed in some other service sectors. My purpose is not to critique the CSO's methods (perhaps, nothing better could be done). Rather, it is to point out the underlying infirmities in the available data in order to generate some healthy doubts when we are confronted with unusual trends.

Or take the 'trade' sector, which accounts for 13.7 per cent of GDP, not much less than the share of all manufacturing! According to Table 11.1, the trade sector grew at a robust 7.3 per cent annual rate in the nineties. GG also say, the rate accelerated in the second half of the decade. How reasonable is this? Remember, growth of commodity sectors had slumped in the latter half of the nineties, imports of non-oil goods were stagnant, inflation was low and a liberalised trade regime was squeezing margins. How does wholesale/retail trade boom in this situation? This certainly calls for more serious research and scrutiny.

More broadly, the methodology of services sector estimates changed significantly in the mid-nineties at the time of transition to the new base year, 1993/94. There is need for serious enquiry to reject the hypothesis that this change in methods may have imparted systematic upward bias to GVA estimates in key service sectors.

So what's going on in services? Plenty. But we need a lot more serious study (in and outside the CSO) to distinguish the real trends from the apparent ones.

Table 11.1

Services in India

Sector	*Per cent share in GDP*			*Average annual growth (%)*		
	1980/81	*1990/91*	*2000/01*	*1950/51-1980/81*	*1980/81-1990/91*	*1990/91-2000/01*
Trade (wholesale /retail)	11.7	11.9	13.7	4.8	5.9	7.3
Hotels and restaurants	0.7	0.7	1.0	4.8	6.5	9.3
Railways	1.5	1.4	1.1	4.2	4.5	3.6
Other transport & storage	3.6	3.8	4.3	6.3	6.3	6.9
Communication (post, telecom)	1.0	1.0	2.0	6.7	6.1	13.6
Banking	1.9	3.4	6.3	7.2	11.9	12.7
Insurance	0.5	0.8	0.7	7.1	10.9	6.7
Dwellings, real estate	4.0	4.8	4.5	2.6	7.7	5.0
Business services	0.2	0.3	1.1	4.2	13.5	19.8
Public administration; defence	5.3	6.0	6.1	6.1	7.0	6.0
Personal services	1.6	1.1	1.1	1.7	2.4	5.0
Community services	4.0	4.3	5.5	4.8	6.5	8.4
Other services	1.1	1.0	0.7	3.4	5.3	7.1
Total services	**37.1**	**40.5**	**48.1**	**4.5**	**6.6**	**7.5**

Source: J. Gordon and P. Gupta (2003). "Understanding India's Services Revolution", November, at *www.imf.org/delhi*, (Based on CSO data).

12

Growth prospects: a reality check

In the last couple of months growth euphoria has been sweeping the media, business associations and government pronouncements. Official estimates of 8 per cent plus GDP growth in 2003/04 have fuelled the optimism. The third quarter (October-December) CSO estimate of 10.4 per cent GDP growth has induced headlines of India being the fastest growing economy in the world. Senior government spokesmen (including the Finance Minister) have been reported to confidently project 8 per cent growth for the next several years. Election pamphlets are promising 10 per cent growth. How serious is all this? Has the Indian economy really attained a new trajectory of sustained 8 per cent growth? I am afraid not, for the reasons spelt out below.

To begin with, let's put the 8.1 per cent growth of 2003/04 in perspective. As Table 12.1 shows, it follows a sluggish 4 per cent rate recorded in 2002/03, coming after a Ninth Plan average growth of 5.5 per cent, which, in turn, reflected a marked slowdown from the reform-driven growth surge of 6.7 per cent experienced in 1992-1997. Much of the economic dynamism of 2003/04 simply reflects an exceptional rebound in agriculture from a drought-affected 5 per cent drop in 2002/03 to a strong 9 per cent recovery thanks to the best monsoon in 20 years. Services also grew strongly and industry did moderately well. If the last two years are averaged, then agriculture reverts to the recent trend of 2 per cent growth and overall GDP shows a healthy but unremarkable 6 per cent increase. No clear evidence of a new 8 per cent growth path here.

Let me turn to the major reasons why India's medium term (next five years) growth is far more likely to be constrained to 6 per cent or below than to rip along at 8 per cent.

Savings-investment

Growth requires investment, which has to be financed by savings. In the past five years, India's investment-GDP ratio has been firmly stuck in the range of 23-24 per cent. This is simply not enough to generate sustained growth of 7 or 8 per cent per year. Economic growth at this pace requires investment ratios of 30 per cent or higher. That's the lesson of the 'miracle economies' of East Asia. Their exceptional growth performance was built on high rates of investment and savings. Actually, private savings of households and companies has done well in India, comparable to East Asian countries. But this good record has been thoroughly undermined by dismal performance of public savings. In the last four years, government dissaving (revenue deficit) has averaged over 6.5 per cent of GDP and shows little sign of serious improvement. With such record levels of dissaving, there is no chance of achieving the national investment rates necessary to propel 8 per cent growth.

Labour force/employment

If capital is one key input for growth, labour is another. The starry-eyed optimists point to the 'demographic dividend' of the country's young population and fast-growing labour force. Yes, there is potential here. But labour has to be employed to produce output. Unfortunately, our track record in generating employment in the last decade has been very weak. Without rapid job growth an expanding labour force ceases to be an asset and becomes a huge social problem. That has already happened and the realistic prospects indicate bigger problems ahead, particularly since much of the future growth in population and labour force will be concentrated in the poor, slow-growing, populous BIMARU states of north India (see *Business Standard*, November 25, 2003 for my detailed arguments). The growth outlook is further clouded by the low standards of education, literacy and health in these laggard states.

And the extreme fiscal weakness of these state governments precludes rapid improvement of social programmes.

External sector

China and several East Asian countries have demonstrated exceptional skill in harnessing foreign trade and investment to propel their rapid economic growth. Put differently, they have been brilliant at making globalisation work for them. We have been much more timid and have reaped much less gain from economic integration with the rest of the world. That we account for only about 0.8 per cent of world exports and about 0.4 per cent the world's foreign direct investment (FDI) inflows testifies to our timidity. Our recent successes with software exports and BPO services underline our potential, just as our long-term, lacklustre performance with manufactured exports points to severe policy failures in nurturing an internationally competitive industrial sector. Politics permitting, our service exports will continue to be a bright spot in our external economic engagement. But without much higher levels of labour-intensive industrial exports and export-oriented FDI, we cannot hope to capture the dynamism of high-growth East Asian economies. The necessary reforms of labour laws, banking, SSI reservations, FDI policies and infrastructure, continue to be impeded by politics and vested interests.

Infrastructure constraints

Well-travelled observers have noted that India has the worst economic infrastructure among all significant emerging market economies in the world. Usually, they are referring to electric power, roads, ports and urban services. They used to include telecom but there we have made real progress in the last decade. We may take some justifiable comfort from the progress on the National Highway Development Programme. But the dismal condition of most state highways and rural roads continues to exact an enormous toll of productivity, growth and jobs in agriculture, industry and exports. As for the power sector, the long history of hugely inefficient SEBs, massive theft, pervasive underpricing to agriculture, declining investment, frequent brownouts and blackouts, are all well-known problems. Unfortunately, knowledge of the problems has not spawned quick and durable solutions. Progress has been incremental and not commensurate with the needs of a high-growth economy. Conversely, without much swifter improvement in power, it is hard to envisage sustained fast growth of industry, especially small and medium units, which cannot afford captive power. If power remains the biggest single infrastructure bottleneck today, water could well be the greatest problem in future.

Agriculture

It is hard to find a fast-growing developing economy where agriculture is not growing at 4 per cent or higher. It may be no accident that during India's fastest 5-year growth spurt (1992-1997), agriculture grew at 4.7 per cent. Since then the trend rate seems to have dropped to around 2 per cent a year, even including the, 9 per cent bonanza of 2003/04. The reasons are many and include, declining public investment by cash-strapped states, grossly inadequate maintenance of irrigation assets, falling water tables, decaying rural roads, unresponsive research and extension services, soil damage from excessive urea use (encouraged by high subsidies) and a distorted incentive structure which impedes diversification from foodgrains. Tackling these problems will take time, money, understanding and political will. Speedy resolutions are simply not in sight. Ergo, nor is a rapid and sustained revival of agriculture, without which 8 per cent GDP growth will remain a chimera.

Services

Can rapid growth of services compensate for slow growth of industry and agriculture? I have repeatedly pointed out why it can't (most recently in *Business Standard,* December 23, 2003). Just look at the table column for 1997-2002 in Table 12.1. Services grew at an unprecedented 8 per cent. Yet the economy grew at only 5.5 per cent in that period. The arithmetic of growth is straightforward. For the entire economy to grow at 8 per cent you can't have half of it growing at less than 4 per cent!

Regional dimension

The Tenth Plan presents a consistent set of projections for the Indian economy to grow at 8 per cent. It shows that the states of Bihar, MP, Rajasthan and UP must grow at 7 per cent or higher (like East Asian 'tiger economies'). The problem is that in the Ninth Plan period they managed average growth of only 4 per cent. The required acceleration strains credibilty.

Then there are growth inhibitors of rising public debt, weakening governance, AIDS...

After all this, dear reader, if you believe India will grow at 8 per cent in the medium term, well...you will believe anything!

Table 12.1

Growth of GDP and major sectors

(Per cent per annum)

	1951/52-1980/81	1981/82-1990/91	1992/93-1996/97	1997/98-2001/02	2002/03	2003/04
GDP	**3.6**	**5.6**	**6.7**	**5.5**	**4.0**	**8.1**
Agriculture	2.5	3.6	4.7	1.9	-5.2	9.1
Industry	5.3	7.1	7.6	4.5	6.4	6.5
Services	4.5	6.7	7.6	8.1	7.1	8.4

Source: CSO.

13

Eight per cent growth forever?

In a paper published in October 2004, I foresaw India's economic growth in the medium-term (say, five years plus) at about 6 per cent, that is, at pretty much the average rate experienced in the last quarter century. A couple of reviewers of the book (and some other interlocutors) have justifiably asked if I still adhere to this somewhat bearish prospect, given the 8 per cent growth performance of the Indian economy in the last three years (2003/04-2005/06). I owe them an answer.

To begin with, let me admit straightaway that I did not expect such strong growth in the last two years (2003/04 was a more predictable, agriculture-led rebound from the drought-affected slump of the previous year). So, as far as the short-term is concerned, I was simply wrong. The only caveat I would enter, is my continued discomfort with the sustained high growth of the services sector (accounting for over 55 per cent of GDP) estimated by CSO. As Table 13.1 shows, the growth of services has averaged 8.5 per cent after 1996/97, compared to 4.5 per cent in the 30 years 1951/52-1980/81, 6.7 per cent in the eighties and 7.6 per cent in the post-reform growth surge of 1992-1997. In contrast, industrial growth has averaged hardly 6 per cent after 1996/97, markedly slower than services and (as I have pointed out on other occasions) quite unusually so, given India's growth history and that of other developing countries. Unusual doesn't make the CSO's estimates incorrect. It just raises doubts (shared by others, such as Prithwis De in *Business Standard*, May 16, 2005), especially when one takes account of the much more indirect methods of estimating services value added deployed by CSO in comparison with the methods used for agriculture and industry. I can't help recalling the pithy remark of a former head of the CSO's national income division on the methods he had to rely on: "If you come into my kitchen, you will never eat my food!"

Putting such nagging doubts to one side, I must freely admit that I had not anticipated either the strength of the global economy or the (linked) longevity of the industrial upswing in India, since 2003. There clearly is a boom in industrial investment and output. The key issue is, will it be sustained? More generally, is 8 per cent economic growth now our inalienable right for the next five years, say, 2006-2011? The pronouncements by government ministers would certainly suggest so. Indeed, rather like the 'India Shining' days of spring 2004, 10 per cent growth ambitions are also wafting in Delhi's dusty, dry air once again, despite the waterless, powerless hardships of the capital's citizens (leaving aside the favoured denizens of Lutyens' inner city).

In assessing the realism of such aspirations, let's take a moment to review recent history. A glance at the table suggests some caution. After the post-reform growth spurt of 1992-1997, averaging an all-time high of 6.7 per cent for five consecutive years, growth in the remaining four years of the nineties slowed to 5.5 per cent. In the next five years (2001-2006) thanks to the unexpected (at least by me) boom of 2004-2006, average growth has climbed back up to the 6.7 per cent record of 1992-1997. Because of the underlying momentum of economic activity (not to mention estimation methods!), this record is likely to be surpassed if we take the five years, 2002-2007. But only marginally; we would still be in the neighbourhood of 7 per cent 'only'. So, two points merit emphasis. First, we have experienced growth deceleration in our recent past and cannot assume immunity from such experience in future. Second, despite the 8 per cent spurt of 2003/04-2005/06, we have yet to surpass the five-year growth record set in 1992-1997.

Past performance is certainly relevant. But my real doubts about sustaining 8 per cent economic growth for the next five years has much more to do with the continuing infirmities of economic policy. In giving a short list of these I will inevitably sound like a broken record (itself a meaningless simile for the digital generation!). First, despite the prolonged and tortuous efforts of successive governments, real progress in relieving the infrastructure bottlenecks of power, roads, water, sanitation and airports remains painfully slow. Second, in spite of some moderation of fiscal deficits in recent years, real interest rates are creeping up, weakening one of the key props of the current investment boom. And future fiscal deficits remain hostage to unchecked expenditure populism and revenue laxity of the kind exemplified by the Special Economic Zones scheme, which could shrink substantially the future tax base. Third, serious underutilisation of our abundant manpower resource seems likely to persist, given the political fondness for dysfunctional labour laws. Indeed, the renewed affection for reservations in jobs is likely to hugely distort labour markets further, to the detriment of productivity, livelihoods and social cohesion. Fourth, after almost a decade of slow growth in agriculture, we seem no nearer to viable solutions. Amongst other things, our policy makers do not seem to understand that the solution to massive underemployment and low labour productivity in agriculture may lie outside the sector: through promoting rapid growth of labour-using manufacturing (shades of labour laws again). Fifth, government still conducts and controls far too much of economic activity in the country, despite the mounting evidence of the costs this imposes. More broadly, continuing slippage in standards of governance all round are exacting a significant (perhaps, rising?) economic toll. Sixth, the government's response to the global challenge of rising energy prices remains woefully inadequate. And I haven't even mentioned the spectres of AIDS, bird flu, global recession or protectionism and other sundry threats which could spin out of control and threaten economic buoyancy.

Against this background, I would not bet on 8 per cent growth for the next five years. Even after taking due account of the demonstrated dynamism and resilience of India's remarkably resourceful people, a growth rate in the range of 6 to 7 per cent seems more likely. If you want to play the game of betting on a particular figure, I suggest an average growth of 6.5 per cent for 2006-2011. Five years hence, if I am still writing this column (not asking for commitments, Mr. Ninan!), I promise to revisit the factual record. In the meantime, I can't resist requoting George Eliot: "Among all forms of mistake, prophecy is the most gratuitous!"

Table 13.1

Growth rate of GDP and major sectors

	1951/52-1980/81	*1981/82-1990/91*	*1992/93-1996/97*	*1997/98-2000/01*	*2001/02-2005/06*
GDP	**3.6**	**5.6**	**6.7**	**5.5**	**6.7**
Agriculture	2.5	3.6	4.7	1.0	2.5
Industry	5.3	7.1	7.6	4.8	7.0
Services	4.5	6.7	7.6	8.5	8.5

Source: CSO; data for 1951/52 to 1999/00 are at 1993/94 prices and for 2000/01 to 2005/06 at 1999/00 prices.

E

Infrastructure problems

14

Foreign exchange for infrastructure, anyone?

India's foreign exchange reserves are burgeoning at about US $ 120 billion, perhaps double the level required by prudential considerations. Key infrastructure sectors are starved of investment, especially public investment. So why not deploy the 'excess' reserves (which earn low returns for the economy) to build much-needed infrastructure facilities and thus boost the country's growth? What could be more obvious? The obvious sometimes invites weird and interesting schemes. Some eight or nine years ago, when we had our first taste of abundant reserves, the Planning Commission (or at least one of its articulate members) had wanted to use the reserves to restructure loss-making public enterprises! Saner counsel prevailed and the proposal was stymied. This time around newspaper reports indicate that the Planning Commission (henceforth, PC) is pushing a more structured scheme to use forex reserves for infrastructure financing. Is this scheme sounder than its predecessor?

First, what seem to be the key elements of the scheme? There is lot of confusing talk of special purpose vehicles and special accounts. Judging by reports, the heart of the proposal seems to be as follows. The government will increase the Centre's fiscal deficit (over and above levels implicit in the Fiscal Responsibility and Budget Management Act) by a specified amount, say, Rs. 20,000 crores a year, to fund worthwhile public infrastructure investment. To ensure that this additional deficit does not raise interest rates and crowd out other investment, the entire amount would be raised by placing an equivalent value of government bonds directly with the Reserve Bank at the prevailing interest rate. Since this constitutes monetisation of the deficit with the potential for increasing money supply and inflation, the new public investment will be structured to be import-intensive. Ideally, if the full 20,000 crores were spent on imports then forex reserves would decline by this amount. In effect, the increase in domestic assets of the RBI (from the additional government bonds) would be fully neutralised by a corresponding decline in foreign assets (reserves), thus leaving the supply of reserve money (and hence, broad money) unchanged.

Abracadabra! The scheme, thus, claims to accomplish 20,000 crore a year (only an illustrative figure) of additional public investment (out of RBI's forex reserves), without fanning inflation and without crowding out other ongoing investment and with only a cosmetic increase in the fiscal deficit. In the likely event that not all of the additional public infrastructure investment will constitute imports, the reports suggest that the government will undertake other measures such as customs duties reductions and/or currency appreciation to bring about the full forex decline required to neutralise the fresh monetised government borrowing.

This seems to be a pretty good deal. But appearances can be deceptive. Its time to raise a few doubts. First, much of infrastructure investment is not import-intensive; for example roads, irrigation and airports. The additional expenditure will not lead to much decline in forex reserves. That means the effect of monetisation will have significant inflationary consequences. As for the suggested measures of customs-duty cuts and currency appreciation, these could (perhaps should?) be done anyway in a context of 'excess reserves'. Their desirability is not linked to RBI-financed government investment. Second, although the suggested option for cutting import duties is reasonable from a trade liberalisation perspective, it does entail revenue loss and hence, a higher fiscal deficit with the usual consequences of pressure on interest rates and crowding out.

Third, while the effects of the higher fiscal deficit entailed by the basic scheme are claimed to be neutralised through monetisation, what about its public debt consequences? In particular, won't there be an increase in India's already high (85 per cent of GDP) and rising public debt to GDP ratio? And won't this lead to a higher debt service burden on government finances?

The adverse signalling consequences of higher fiscal deficits (even if monetised) and rising public debt ratios should not be underestimated. Fourth, nor should the trajectory of FRBM targets for various fiscal ratios be lightly tampered with. Especially not to accommodate the government's own scheme, as distinct from unforeseen shocks and contingencies. Public investment in infrastructure should be increased, but through the normal methods of raising more tax and non-tax revenue resources and containing low priority current expenditures.

Fifth, there is something distinctly odd about suspending normal practices for managing the government's borrowing requirements and undertaking *ad hoc* placement of the illustrative 20,000 crores infrastructure-financing-bond directly with RBI. Surely the conduct of public debt, interest and liquidity management policies of the RBI should not be hostage to specific components of government expenditure? Isn't macroeconomic policy all about aggregates? Must we encumber it with a typically Indian proclivity for dubious special cases? If a special modality is constructed for this case, might there not be many other competing claimants for special dispensation for freedom from the fiscal constraints of the FRBM?

Talking of special expenditure components and their right to elaborate special treatment, it is more than a little disquieting that the best examples of sizable government expenditure, which have the property of debiting wholly on abundant forex reserves, is provided by purchases of imported military aircraft, ships, tanks and other large-ticket defence systems. The PC's well-intentioned proposals for special modalities for public infrastructure financing could invite enthusiastic attention from the nation's service chiefs.

They could readily advocate that monetised, debt-financing of defence imports will have no inflationary consequences as the extent of monetisation will be swiftly offset by the decline in forex reserves!

Seventh, the PC's proposed scheme assumes that the public infrastructure investments will yield high returns to the economy? Hence, the justification for elaborate special treatment. But what is the surety for this? Will state electricity boards and public works and irrigation departments suddenly become lean, mean profit centres for government finances just because RBI bends prevailing rules and practices to accommodate a set of special infrastructure financing government bonds? Surely, the opposite is just as likely if not more. Namely, the more the institutions for public infrastructure spending, operation and maintenance are relieved of pressing budget constraints, the more lax they will become in using public funds.

Indeed, is finance the real constraint to higher infrastructure investments? A compelling case could be made (and has been by many, including the PC in the Tenth Plan) that the major obstacles to more high-quality infrastructure investment are embedded in the uncertain regulatory frameworks of key sectors and the rampant populism that pervades policies and practices of major public entities providing infrastructure services. It is these that have to be reformed to transform the quality and quantity of public infrastructure services in India and nudge the country to a higher growth path.

As for the 'problem of excess reserves', the real answer may lie with reviving serious economic reforms (of labour laws, banking, privatisation, SSI reservations, taxation, etc.) that catalyse a sustained revival of industrial investment, which will generate rapid growth of non-oil imports. Till then, the high international prices for oil are doing their bit to contain India's forex reserves.

15

A tale of three cities

A couple of weeks ago, I revisited Dhaka after a gap of many years. I was frankly astonished by the bustle and dynamism of this vibrant, fast-growing metropolis of 14 million inhabitants. It was a far cry from the provincial town of early 1970s, that had lingered in my memory. Nor did I please my relatives and friends in Kolkata, on the journey back, by commenting on the contrast between Dhaka's commercial and construction boom with its gleaming new towers *versus* the relative stagnation and crumbling old buildings of Kolkata. That Kolkata seemed like a commercial backwater after Dhaka was a distinctly uncomfortable reversal of the comparison that had prevailed for over two centuries.

Of course, there are many reasons explaining the different trajectories of these two populous Bengali metropolises. In the 34 years since Bangladesh's independence, Dhaka has gained enormously from being the nation's capital city, favoured by endless government construction contracts and other forms of government patronage. In contrast, Kolkata lost her political privileges with the shift of the British imperial capital to Delhi way back in 1912. Then came the Partition of 1947, which, at one stroke, idled Kolkata's jute mills, extinguished the property rights of the city's *zamindars* and spawned a flood of impoverished refugees from East Bengal. To make matters worse, the ill-conceived freight-equalisation scheme of Nehruvian, socialist planners, thoroughly undermined the comparative advantage of steel-based industries in the Bengal-Bihar region and led to the 'sickening' of numerous Kolkata-based engineering industries.

Kolkata's accumulating industrial-commercial woes cannot be all attributed to acts of high (or low?) politics and stupid central planning beyond West Bengal's control. The Naxalite insurgency of the early 1970s and three decades of deteriorating investment climate under the Left Front government led to massive capital flight (often to western India) and a highly unproductive labour-industry culture. It is precisely during these three recent decades that Dhaka's industry (especially, garments and textiles) has come of age, unconstrained by Kolkata's politically strong labour unions and dysfunctional labour laws. In 1980, Bangladesh exported less than a hundred million dollars of clothing and textiles. Last year such exports were close to six billion dollars! Much of this thriving new industry is located in and around Dhaka, pumping zillions of takas into the city's economy, fuelling a sustained retail boom, driving property prices skywards and choking the city's streets with lakhs of new cars.

Yes, wages of garment workers are often low and job security is limited. But it's a lot better than available alternatives. And with nearly 90 per cent of such workers being female, there is a major process of female empowerment underway. When coupled with Bangladesh's justly renowned revolution in micro-credit institutions in rural areas and large-scale NGO-led initiatives in education and health, the dimensions of social transformation seem decidedly more impressive than what has happened across the border in West Bengal. New studies of trends in education, health, nutrition and demographic parameters support this impression.

Dhaka's headlong growth is not without problems. Those familiar with South Asian cities will easily recognise the usual litany of woes: unplanned urban development, unscrupulous builder lobbies, mounting traffic congestion, inadequate water and sanitation infrastructure, power shortages and (perhaps, more than in other South Asian metropolises) rising urban crime. Municipal finance and governance is probably even weaker than in Kolkata or Mumbai, though the weaknesses are partially masked (as in Delhi) by the favouritism (in finance and other support systems) extended by the central government.

This tale was supposed to cover three cities. Well, two fortnights ago, on the fateful Tuesday of July 26 , I joined (involuntarily) lakhs of *Mumbaikars* in wading through waist-deep water (or should I say sewage?) during the floods which swept the (always) far-fetched dreams of rivalling Shanghai down clogged city drains and potholed, waterlogged streets. Much has since been written on what needs to be done to save Mumbai, including: clearing the natural waterways of illegal constructions, improving non-existent disaster-management systems, revamping municipal governance and allocating central and state funds to improve the city's dying urban infrastructure.

These remedies are sensible enough. But perhaps they neglect two broader themes which are critical for the health of South Asian cities. A large part of Mumbai's urban malaise stems from the decades-old demise of her textile industries. True, various service activities have flourished including finance and commerce. But nothing has quite replaced the 'blue-collar' workforce of Mumbai's mills. It's similar to the problems of Kolkata where no major labour-using industry has developed to replace the economic base generated by jute mills and engineering industries. The contrast with Dhaka is striking. There, the millions of jobs created by the burgeoning new textiles/garments have provided a large part of the sinews for urban growth. Indeed, the same is true for the flourishing urban centres of Coastal China and South-East Asia: the growth of prosperous cities is intimately linked with the rise of labour-intensive industries.

In this crucial domain, our archaic and inflexible labour laws continue to choke the creation of millions of good jobs in labour-using industries. India has hardly 5 million formal sector jobs in manufacturing out of a labour force of over 350 million! In contrast, Chinese factories employ well over 100 million workers (over 150 million by some estimates). It's these blue-collar jobs that can provide the economic lifeblood of healthy urban growth, whether in

Kolkata or Mumbai. So, reform of our labour laws is necessary not only to stave off the real prospects of unemployment nightmares, but also to regenerate our failing metropolises.

The second broad (and neglected) theme for urban regeneration in India is the revamping of municipal property tax systems (and the associated reform of rent control laws). It's a dull subject, but it lies at the core of successful cities (Dhaka, you need this too). Cities need urban infrastructure and the most durable way of raising such funds is to tax equitably those who own the city's residential and commercial buildings and enjoy the benefits of urban infrastructure. Disaster-triggered subventions from central and state governments are welcome but they are not a reliable source of long-term revenue in the way that a well-functioning property tax system is.

So my two-fold *mantra* for urban regeneration in India is reform of labour laws and property tax systems. Hello, is anybody listening?

16

India's water troubles

Official and demi-official reports from national and international organisations are a dime a dozen these days. If there is only one report you have time to read in the next three months, then I recommend "India's Water Economy: Bracing for a Turbulent Future" (IWE, for short), written by a team headed by the World Bank's senior water advisor, John Briscoe, and drawing substantially on a dozen background papers by Indian scholars and practitioners such as Ramesh Bhatia, George Varughese, Tushaar Shah, Sebastian Morris, Nirmal Mohanty and Vijay Vyas. The final draft is available at *www.worldbank.org.in.* Why do I pick this report from the zillion others that float across my desk? Yes, it's cogent, well-written, marshals a tremendous range of information and analysis and puts it across in an accessible, user-friendly format. But perhaps above all, because IWE is about water, something that affects us all...and is likely to do so increasingly as this precious fluid becomes steadily more scarce for all of India's citizens, in large part because of our collective failure to manage water systems well.

In this brief column I can't hope to do justice to the rich analysis in IWE and its well-nuanced advocacy for a charter of water sector reforms. I can only offer a 'trailer' by summarising some of the key messages and themes of diagnosis and prescription that are on offer. It's no substitute for reading this excellent report.

India has always faced a severe water management challenge with its highly seasonal pattern of rainfall, resulting in 50 per cent of precipitation in just 15 days and 90 per cent of river flows in only four months. Massive investments in water storage, control and distribution were clearly warranted. In the century or so up to around 1970, British and Indian water engineers undertook major projects of dams, canals and municipal water systems, which brought rapid economic development to the once-arid north-west India and large parts of the Deccan. Such investments in water infrastructure spearheaded major advances in food security and hydro-power production. They also played a crucial role in generating rural development and reducing poverty, not least through enormously augmented demand for labour on irrigated farm lands.

Despite these water investments, India's dams can only store about 200 cubic metres per person, compared to around 1000 cubic meters per capita in China, Mexico and South Africa. What's more, the likely effects of global climate change will lead to greater storage needs to manage more variable glacier melt and more variable monsoons. One important message of IWE is a call for much greater investment in dams and reservoirs, in contrast to the World Bank's 1990s opposition to big dams (fanned partly by the shrill advocacy of a set of international and national anti-development NGOs).

The second major problem relates to the woeful maintenance of the water infrastructure assets created by 1970. For a variety of reasons (not adequately explained in IWE) the systems of maintenance and operation of public water infrastructure went into steady decline from around the 1960s. The familiar litany of woes grew: low user charges, poor accountability, endemic corruption, massive over-staffing preempting meagre finances and a generally bureaucratic and unresponsive approach to water users. The mounting backlog of deferred maintenance and crumbling assets earned Indian water investment strategy the unflattering sobriquet of "Build-Neglect-Rebuild!"

Rural and urban water problems would have assumed crisis proportions long ago but for the advent of the new 'transformational technology' of tube wells around the 1960s. Faced with malfunctioning public water systems, farmers and urban dwellers switched massively to tube wells to meet with their mounting water needs. IWE estimates that today 70 per cent of irrigation needs and 80 per cent of domestic water supplies in India are met through pumping up groundwater through tube wells. But this massively deployed private response to public failure can only be temporary. Water tables are plummeting and aquifers are running dry. Estimates show that 15 per cent of aquifers are already critical and the number is projected to rise to 60 per cent in a couple of decades. The consequences of such water stress are simply unimaginable, especially since the phenomenon of aquifer depletion is concentrated in the most populated and economically productive areas of the country. In a word, the usual Indian ploy of 'muddling through' is simply unsustainable.

So what's to be done? There is no single magic bullet. But the broad outlines of a recuperative strategy seems clear. First, state agencies and water users have to work together to bring aquifer withdrawals in line with recharge. Simply passing laws and regulations won't work. They have to be buttressed by systems of tradable water entitlements, credible user associations and a creative approach to pricing and incentives. Second, with the obvious limitations on groundwater, there will have to be much greater reliance on surface water systems, both through recuperation of existing, undermaintained systems and also through 'large-scale investment in public infrastructure' of new dam systems, canals, municipal distribution networks and wastewater treatment plants.

Third, and perhaps above all, "it is going to require a dramatic transformation in the way in which public water services are provided to farmers, households and industries, in which the watchwords are water entitlements, financial sustainability, accountability, competition, regulation and entry of alternatives to government provision including cooperatives and the private sector." If all that sounds to you like higher prices for water from formal systems, you heard right. It would be absurd to imagine that an increasingly scarce and valuable resource can be intelligently managed without significant recourse to prices and markets.

On the path to reform, beware of all those well-heeled celebrities who will resist change in the name of the poor. Just remember two things: first, today's massive subsidies are enjoyed not by the poor but by those, who actually consume most of the water and electricity, namely the well-off farmers and town-dwellers, including the anti-reform celebrities from up-market city areas. Second, the poor typically pay huge prices today to water vendors and other intermediaries. Reforms which augment water supply and give some real substance to the entitlements of the poor are much more likely to benefit them.

Can the broad strategy of reform, outlined by IWE, actually work? I certainly hope so. Otherwise the future is too fearsome to contemplate!

F

Budget and tax policies

17

The good, the bad and the ugly

When I agreed to a suggestion to review the recent 'Mini-Budget' (henceforth, MB) of the NDA government, I didn't realise that MB referred to an ongoing process rather than a one-off event! The sop story goes on...and on, seemingly without end. For manageability, if nothing else, I shall confine my appraisal to the major announcements made in the fortnight between January 8 and 22. I shall also sidestep the very important issue of the legitimacy of making budget-type policy announcements on the eve of a general election and during a Parliamentary recess, other than to note that the MB clearly breaches (at least, in spirit) the long-established conventions of restraint on such matters.

To begin at the beginning (much easier to find than the end!), let's start with the tax measures announced on January 8. The unquestionably 'good' part of the MB is the reduction in the 'peak' import duty on non-agricultural goods to 20 per cent (from 25 per cent) and the abolition of the special additional duty (SAD) of 4 per cent. These measures are genuine acts of unilateral trade liberalisation that economists have long advocated and merit full support. They are also consistent with the government's announced strategy of reducing customs duties 'to East Asian levels' to promote better integration with the world economy, in general, and the dynamic East-Asian economies, in particular. The measures are all the more praiseworthy since they do not pander to any populist lobby. Most Indians believe (wrongly) that import duties are borne by foreigners and so reducing duties helps them, not residents.

Actually, of course, lower duties benefit consumers/buyers of imports and exporters. They also spur productivity improvements in protected industries.

The NDA government has been reasonably consistent in gradually reducing peak import duties and opening up to foreign investment (including the recent relaxation of equity caps in some sectors). In these important dimensions there has been substantial continuity (of external policies) with the major liberalisations undertaken by the Congress government of 1991-1996. This is all the more remarkable (and welcome) when these policy actions are juxtaposed against the inward-looking 'swadeshi' rhetoric of the BJP election manifesto of early 1998. Full credit must go to the PM and successive FMs for managing this delicate transition.

The import duty changes in the MB are by no means flawless. For one thing, they do not fulfil the earlier promise to cluster all import duties into two bands of 20 per cent and 10 per cent, let alone the economists' recommendation for a single, unified customs duty rate. Second, as in the last budget for 2003/04, there is a great deal of unnecessary and unsound tinkering with many duty rates to favour some industry or the other. Third, the engineering and capital goods industries once again get short shrift, with duty rates reduced well below the rates applied to their main inputs, such as steel. The result is negative protection for these crucial industries at just the time when demand for investment goods might be picking up. Leaving aside old slogans of 'self-reliance' and 'swadeshi', the playing field is tilted against these industries.

What is 'bad' about the MB's tax measures is the failure to broaden the revenue base of either central excise or income taxes. As various tax-reform committees and analysts have pointed out, the steady (and desirable) reduction in distortive customs duties and revenues needed to be compensated through effective broadening of the base for the other major central taxes, notably excise, income and company taxation. This has become increasingly urgent against the backdrop of a falling tax-GDP ratio and very high fiscal deficits. But there is not even a whiff in the MB of the exemption-cutting recommendations of the Kelkar task forces of yesteryear. Indeed, like the previous budget (for 2003/04), the MB takes the opposite, retrograde tack of shrinking the tax base through more exemptions, for example for DVDs and VCDs. The crucial importance of the unified 16 per cent CENVAT rate (supported by additional special excises on a few luxury commodities), achieved substantially by Yashwant Sinha, was seriously undermined in the last budget by the legitimisation of a concessional 8 per cent rate. The MB aggravates this error by reducing the excise on computers and aviation fuel to 8 per cent (if computers merit concessional treatment, why not most other goods?). Similarly, the waiver of income tax filing obligations for certain categories, weakens the base of income taxation. Jaswant seems to be rolling back some of Yashwant's tax reforms!

So much for the 'good' and the 'bad.' What about the 'ugly?' Well, perhaps that's too strong a word (I couldn't resist the title of the old Clint Eastwood movie classic). 'Unsound' or 'unfortunate' may be more appropriate descriptions for the MB's spawning of huge new 'funds' for spending on agri-infrastructure (Rs. 50,000 crore), small-medium industry (Rs. 10,000 crore), infrastructure/manufacturing (Rs. 50,000 crore), urban amenities for rural areas and what have you. As far as I can make out from the terse and confusing press notes announcing these initiatives, they boast some common features. First, they are a trifle vague on where the money is going to come from; there is talk of 'capital markets and budgetary resources'. Second, they will be managed by existing financial intermediaries: NABARD, SIDBI, IDBI, IDFC, etc. Third, they all involve subsidised lending to the concerned beneficiaries, typically at an interest rate 2 per cent below the prime lending rate. Fourth, government will, in all cases, underpin the operations through budgetary support or guarantees or both.

If these initiatives are serious, they can inflict serious damage on our already precarious fiscal situation (third largest fiscal deficit in the world, 85 per cent government debt-to-GDP ratio and all that) and further weaken the strained balance sheets of some of our major financial intermediaries. Our own financial history (and that of many other countries) demonstrates how large-scale subsidised lending, undermines the viability of banks and other financial intermediaries and destroys the banking and credit culture. They also provide fertile breeding grounds for crony-lending and other scams. Ultimately, the imprudence spawns large balance sheet holes which have to be filled by budgetary transfers (recall UTI, IFCI, RRBs, banks...). Against this background, it's puzzling how such half-baked schemes continue to proliferate. Perhaps, the eternal (and unsound) appeal of interest subsidies is the prospect of leveraging large flows at 'small' upfront budget cost. Such myopia ignores the huge capitalised cost of interest subsidies and the major damage to efficiency and probity of concerned financial intermediaries. It's also puzzling how the MB's schemes passed screening by RBI. Or was that venerable institution not consulted by the Leviathan? Or overruled?

Perhaps these 'fundy' schemes are not meant to be taken seriously? After all, who remembers the last budget's Rs. 60,000 crore 'thrust to infrastructure' which was to be leveraged through 'viability gap funding' of only Rs. 2000 crore from the budget? My prediction then that there was likely to be more 'gap' and less 'viability' appears to have come true. But the announcement of non-serious schemes (even on the eve of elections) is not costless. They divert a great deal of administrative energy from government's serious spending programmes and policy efforts. They breed widespread cynicism about public policy. They also undermine the credibility of Central Government, at a juncture when this scarce resource is vital for the nation's long-term health.

Bottom-line: the (ongoing!) Mini-Budget has some good parts, some bad parts and some...er...unsound/unfortunate parts.

18

Tax policies for 2005

Yes, it's that time of year again, when every self-respecting columnist feels obliged to tender fiscal policy advice to the Finance Minister and his overworked colleagues in the ministry. Well, who am I to shirk obligations? I shall limit my comments to the tax policy side of the budget.

First, at the risk of repetition, let's briefly review some contextual background. Thirty years of global tax reform have been dominated by a handful of big themes. First, corporate profits should be taxed at a flat, moderate rate (in the range of 25 to 35 per cent), with the tax base being as free of exemptions and incentives as possible. Similarly, personal income tax rates should be modest, with revenue buoyancy being sought by broadening the tax base through good compliance and minimal exemptions. Some progressivity in rates remains the norm, despite the growing debate on flat rate taxes. Third, customs tariffs should be low and, preferably, at an uniform rate across commodities to promote sound trade policy. Fourth, a single rate VAT up to the retail stage is the preferred form of domestic taxation of goods and services. Finally, a modern, IT-based tax administration is seen as a central requirement for a good tax system.

Ever since V.P. Singh's *Long Term Fiscal Policy* (1985) and the Chelliah *Tax Reform Committee Report* (1991/92) these big themes have also guided efforts at tax reform in India. There has been substantial, if slow, progress, occasionally marred by some backsliding. What should be done in the coming budget? Before giving some suggestions, organised by the major central taxes, one more contextual remark is in order. Against a background of high fiscal deficits, soaring government debt, ambitious expenditure programmes and the legal requirement (embodied in the FRBM Act) to reduce fiscal and revenue deficits, I assume that such suggestions should ideally be revenue enhancing or, at worst, revenue neutral. More bluntly, we shouldn't assume that tax reform only means reductions in tax rates!

Central excise

The gradual move towards a single rate (16 per cent) CENVAT for all goods in a production chain, buttressed by additional special excises for a small number of luxury (income elastic) consumer goods, had been a labourious endeavour on the part of successive finance ministers through the 1990s, culminating in the Yashwant Sinha budgets of 1999 and 2000. Since then, and particularly with the Jaswant Singh budget of 2003, there has been a loss of focus, with that budget outlining a triple rate excise structure (8, 16 and 24) and failing to distinguish between the CENVAT rate and (additional) special excises. As experience has shown, the legitimisation of the 8 per cent rate (as anything other than a temporary way station for goods being progressively moved up to the 16 per cent CENVAT) invites continuous lobbying for commodities to be moved down to this rate. Moreover, the propensity to grant outright excise exemptions to various products has increased, undermining the basic logic of the VAT chain. In the last two budgets alone, computers, bicycles, tableware, toys, tractors, dairy machinery, hand tools and mosaic tiles have been totally exempted from excise for less than compelling reasons.

The coming budget needs to reemphasise the centrality and (near) universality of the 16 per cent CENVAT rate by critically reviewing the present long list of products with full exemptions or concessional rates. Nor does it have to shy away from levying (additional) special excises at 8 per cent or higher on a limited range of consumer luxury products. Not, at least, if raising revenue in a non-distortive manner is a serious objective.

There have been repeated attempts to bring the hugely important, but fragmented, textile industry into the CENVAT system. The last attempt by Jaswant Singh in 2003, appeared to be reversed in Chidambaram's 2004 budget. The issue merits revisiting. The guiding consideration should be, what kind of tax system will most help the Indian textile industry to compete successfully in the post-MFA world.

More generally, central excise revenues have shown disturbingly low growth in recent years, at rates well below the growth of output value in manufacturing. The politically sensitive exemptions for small-scale industry cannot be the main reason (there is a separate and obvious economic argument for whittling those down). More likely, there is urgent need to modernise the administration of central excise and find ways of checking the abuse of the CENVAT credit procedures.

Customs duties

During its six-year tenure, the NDA government reduced 'peak' customs tariffs from 40 per cent to 20 per cent. However, the number of commodities (especially agricultural) with tariff rates higher than the 'peak' has grown over this period and needs review. The trade policy case for further reductions of customs tariffs 'to ASEAN levels' remains strong. But for revenue reasons, the decline has to be gradual. Actually, there is still substantial dispersion of tariff rates between zero and 20 per cent. It should be possible (and desirable) to reduce the peak rate to 15 per cent, while raising all (or most) unbound rates below 10 per cent to that level, without any loss of customs revenue. Revenue could also be augmented by pruning the very large number of exemptions (often varied by end-use), which today complicates hugely the customs tariff structure.

According to press reports, the Lahiri committee on taxation of petroleum products has recommended continuation of a significant gap between the tariffs on oil products and the (lower) one on crude oil. If so, this is a pity as it perpetuates the grant of heavy effective protection to the low value-added petroleum refining industry. There was a time in the mid-1990s, when these rates were broadly unified. The economic case for reunification in the coming budget is strong.

Direct taxes

The personal income tax structure has become opaque after the last budget's attempt to relieve taxable income up to 100,000 from any tax without altering the existing exemption limit of 50,000 or the slab structure. In effect, the 10 per cent rate for the slab 50,000 to 60,000 has become redundant. And the curve of marginal tax rates has acquired curious kinks. A cleaner, more transparent structure would be to raise the exemption limit to 75,000, apply the 10 per cent rate to a slab 75,000 to 100,000, a 20 per cent rate to the bracket of 1 to 2 lakh, 30 per cent to the range 2 to 10 lakh and introduce a new rate of 35 per cent for taxable incomes above 10 lakh. This is not really a new slab given that those earning more than 8.5 lakh are already paying a marginal rate of 33 per cent because of the surcharge.

This proposal would have the important added benefit of equalising the top personal income tax rate with the general corporate rate and thus, encourage present non-corporate business forms (like partnerships) to corporatise.

The present general rate of 35 per cent for companies is reasonable and should be retained. The real challenge is to reduce the large number of exemptions for various sectors and kinds of income, which today reduce the effective average rate of company taxation to below 25 per cent. Tinkering with the MAT may help but it could easily be counterproductive.

Our current taxation of capital and capital gains defies economic logic and breaches basic notions of equity. But the structure has been jerked around six times in the last eight years! For that reason alone, I would let it be.

Finally, beware schemes for voluntary disclosure and 'using black money productively'. They reward the dishonest, undermine compliance and rarely augment public revenues in a genuine and durable way.

None of the above is the stuff of 'dream budgets'. But perhaps these suggestions reduce the risks of the real nightmare taxes... low growth and inflation.

19

India's tax reformers

Recently, I had occasion to review India's tax reforms over the past 30 years or so. It's a fascinating story and I thought I would share a few highlights with readers. Today, as we struggle to roll back patently bad taxes, such as the cash withdrawal tax and the new fringe benefit tax, we may forget how far we have travelled since the 1970s, when our tax system was really messed up. And we may fail to accord due credit to the stalwarts of Indian tax reform.

Back then, customs duties were often above 200 per cent on many products. Excise duties ranged between 2 and 100 per cent spread across 24 different rates, not counting much higher duties on tobacco and petroleum and many specific (that is, per unit) duties. Inputs were routinely taxed and credit on taxation of inputs was rare. So 'cascading' of taxes was the norm. Direct taxes were even more bizarre. In 1973/74, the personal income tax boasted 11 different slabs with rates ranging from 10 to 85 per cent. With a surcharge of 15 per cent, the top marginal rate was effectively 97.75. Thus, for every additional 100 rupees earned you got to keep just over 2 rupees! Actually since all wealth was also taxed at significant rates, the cumulative incidence of income and wealth taxes frequently exceeded 100 per cent. The predictable result was widespread evasion and avoidance. Many of the investment companies that today figure prominently in battles for corporate control, owe their genesis to the confiscatory tax regime of the 1970s. Company taxes were typically around 60 per cent and varied across equity-holding patterns. Tax administration was equally complex and arbitrary.

The retreat from these stratospheric (and totally counter-productive) personal income tax rates began in 1974/75, following the Wanchoo Direct Taxes Enquiry Committee Report of 1971. But it was an unsteady descent, with significant reversals during the Janata government years of 1977-1980. Indeed, in 1979/80, Charan Singh raised the tax on net wealth to an unprecedented peak of 5 per cent.

Moden tax reform was really launched in India by V.P. Singh during his brief two years as Finance Minister in 1985-87. For a start, he and his team took a holistic view of the tax system, both direct and indirect. Second, tax reform was driven explicitly by the objectives of economic efficiency, policy stability and equity, not just by the thirst for revenue. Third, for the first time, V.P. Singh articulated a medium-term strategy for tax reform and placed the 'Long Term Fiscal Policy' in Parliament. Fourth, there was a conscious effort to deploy rule-based, fiscal policies in place of discretionary physical controls in the task of economic management. Finally, there was a serious attempt to improve tax administration.

In his first budget, for 1985/86, V. P. Singh reduced the number of income tax slabs from eight to four, cut the top marginal income tax rate to 50 per cent (from 62 per cent), lowered the basic company tax rate also to 50 per cent and abolished estate duty. In the following year, he took another huge stride forward by introducing Modvat (credit for tax paid on inputs) into much of the excise tariff structure, thus ushering in the age of VAT principles into Indian commodity taxation.

With V.P. Singh' s exit from the finance ministry in early 1987, tax reform went into hibernation. Until another Singh, Manmohan, took the lonely helm in 1991. In his five full budgets between 1991 and 1996, especially the ones for 1992/93 and 1994/95, Manmohan Singh joined the exclusive pantheon of India's tax reformers. He reduced income tax slabs to three (20, 30 and 40 per cent), lowered the basic corporate tax rate to 40 per cent, virtually abolished the wealth tax (by exempting financial assets from its purview), did a major clean-up of indirect tax exemptions, extended Modvat to almost the entire manufacturing sector, reduced the number of excise rates and introduced services taxation. Perhaps, his greatest contribution was the reduction of peak customs duties from well above 200 per cent when he came in, to 50 per cent before he left. Duties on investment goods and key intermediates were cut more sharply. By these measures, Singh wrought a sea change in India's hitherto highly restrictive foreign trade policy.

The momentum of Manmohan Singh's tax reforms was largely sustained by Chidambaram and Yashwant Sinha in the remainder of the 1990s, though some might argue that Chidambaram's further reductions in direct tax rates were unjustified in a poor country struggling to raise tax revenues. To Yashwant Sinha must go the credit for the major breakthrough in reforming excise rates, when he conflated 11 excise rates to 3 (in 1999/00) and then, finally, to the single CENVAT rate of 16 per cent in 2000/01 (buttressed by a couple of additional special excises on a few consumer luxuries). All three finance ministers of the nineties (and Jaswant Singh, later) extended central government support to the reform and harmonisation of state sales taxes, culminating in the current transition to state VATs.

If these men (especially V.P. Singh and Manmohan Singh) were the principal tax reformers among finance ministers, who were the key technocrats in the story of Indian tax reform? Pride of place must go to two men who kept alive the idea of serious tax reform in the difficult decades. The first was L.K. Jha, perhaps the most accomplished econocrat of his generation of ICS officials. He chaired the Indirect Taxation Enquiry Committee, whose report of 1978 laid the foundation of the Modvat reforms implemented in V.P. Singh's time. A prominent member of that committee was professor Raja Chelliah, who later came to be widely respected as India's leading public finance authority. As chairman of the Economic Administration Reforms Commission of the early 1980s, Jha also produced important reports on tax policy and administration, which underpinned V.P. Singh's direct tax reforms. Not coincidentally, Chelliah also served on this commission.

Chelliah went on to head the famous Tax Reforms Committee (TRC) of 1991/92. Its three volumes were widely (and rightly) acclaimed as the most comprehensive and analytical treatment of Indian tax policy and reform issues since Independence. The TRC's recommendations guided the policy actions of all three finance ministers (and their senior officials) of the nineties decade. An influential member of the TRC was Amaresh Bagchi, who belongs to that rare and vanishing species of income tax official turned public finance scholar. Later, in 1994, he and his team at the National Institute of Public Finance and Policy, produced a classic study of domestic trade taxes in India. This became a key report guiding the reform of state sales taxes and exploring the VAT options available under India's Constitution.

There were others, including: Govinda Rao whose expert group report of 2001, formed the basis for the recent integration of services taxation with goods taxation under Modvat; Partha Shome whose 2001 report updated the TRC's recommendations; and the various Vijay Kelkar task force reports. These last contained some controversial recommendations. But the reports did resurrect the TRC's emphasis on reducing exemptions and on reforming tax administration. The most recent report also makes a persuasive case for a nationwide, integrated dual-VAT across central and state governments.

We have indeed come a very long way from the 1970s tax jungle. And we owe a deep debt of gratitude to a small band of dedicated tax reformers for guiding us out of those dense, productivity-sapping thickets.

20

The year of bad taxes

Between July 2004 and May 2005 the UPA government has presented and enacted two union budgets. Regrettably, the 'dream team' of Manmohan Singh, P. Chidambaram and Montek Ahluwalia have, in the process, introduced three rank bad taxes and somewhat derailed the train of modern Indian tax reform flagged off by V. P. Singh in 1985. I should probably let Montek off the hook since, in our budget process, the Planning Commission plays no role in budget tax policy. But, as all well-informed people know, the Prime Minister and Finance Minister are the two most important architects of tax policy innovations introduced through budgets. So the buck stops with them. In some ways this is particularly disheartening for tax reformers, since both the present incumbents have (or had?) considerable reputations as tax reformers, especially Manmohan Singh (of 1991-1996 vintage). The three new taxes I am referring to are, of course, the Securities Transaction Tax (STT), the Fringe Benefit Tax (FBT) and the Banking Cash Transactions Tax (BCTT). The first was introduced in 2004 and the latter two in 2005.

Before I say a few words about each of these unfortunate tax experiments and what should now be done with them, I should note that they run counter to some of major themes of our tax reforms in the last two decades, dominated by V.P. Singh in the 1980s and Manmohan Singh in the 1990s (at some risk of over-simplification—and misinterpretation—you could call them two decades of Singh-Singh tax reforms!). These themes include: a thrust towards greater simplicity and transparency in the tax structure; a shift towards taxing value added instead of turnover; the reduction of complex tax rules pregnant with the possibility of discretionary abuse; and a striving for greater equity in the tax structure and its incidence. To a greater or lesser extent, each of the three new taxes go against the grain of these broad and good themes.

The STT of 2004, is a turnover tax on financial transactions, introduced (incongruously) at a time when taxation of value added is replacing turnover taxes in central and state taxation of commodities. Not only does it run counter to the general movement towards value-added taxes but it also breaches the public finance canon against taxing financial transactions (and thus, mucking up the efficiency and development of financial intermediation). A major motivation for its introduction was to substitute for hard-to-collect taxes on short- and long-term capital gains on stock market transactions. If that remains an important justification, I would suggest the following modifications: halve the rates of STT (which will reduce the efficiency costs but retain the alleged informational benefits for tax authorities); double the present rate on short-term equity capital gains from 10 to 20 per cent (thus, bringing it closer to rates on capital gains from other assets); and raise the rate on long-term equity capital gains from zero to 10 per cent (surely more equitable than a complete exemption, especially in a regime where dividends are also tax free in recipients' hands). These suggested changes would reduce efficiency losses, enhance equity (in the sense of fairness) and increase revenue. And the Left should find it easy to support these changes.

The strictures against taxing financial transactions also apply to the BCTT introduced in 2005. The tax was justified as a measure to check evasion and black money generation. This is rather odd since the tax is likely to have the opposite effect of inducing black money operators to stay away from the banking system and conduct their operations purely in cash. If revenue was the objective then the BCTT has been an abject failure, having raised a derisory Rs. 89 crore in the first half of 2005/06. Such taxes also set very bad examples to state governments. Under these circumstances, the best solution would be to simply withdraw this bad and ineffective tax.

The tax which has been opposed the most is the FBT. The criticisms have been strong and largely justified. First, contrary to the finance ministry's claims, the FBT does tax legitimate business expenses, such as sales promotion, telephones usage and business travel. Second, like all presumptive taxes, its burden on businesses is uneven and unfair. Third, in practice, it is a complicated tax. Any tax which requires a 40 page explanatory circular (of the kind issued by the finance ministry in August 2005) cannot be simple! The proliferation of special dispensations and rates for particular categories of expenses for specified industries (and there will be more of them if the tax stays) also adds to complexity and arbitrary incidence. Fourth, the application of the tax imposes a lot more paperwork and administrative costs on businesses. Fifth, such a complex tax is likely to spawn a large amount of discretionary abuse. Finally, the revenue yield does not seem to be substantial: collections in the first half of 2005/06 were only Rs. 822 crore according to the finance ministry's *Mid-year Review* (under the Fiscal Responsibility Act) issued last month. Indeed, as this newspaper has commented editorially (January 12), the FBT encourages companies to reduce the effective tax rate by paying more to employees in the form of perks.

The present Finance Minister used to portray the ideal of gently extracting revenue from taxpayers through the imagery of a bee sipping nectar from a flower. By this analogy, the FBT would seem to be a very large and fearsome bumble bee chewing remorselessly on shrinking violets! Not surprisingly, various industry associations have proposed schemes for exemption from the FBT in return for paying a company tax higher by 1 or 2 per cent than the general rate of 30 per cent. I recall Rahul Bajaj offering such a 'trade' in a TV panel discussion on budget day last February. Going forward, this seems to be an eminently sensible approach: abolish the FBT and raise the company tax rate by a per cent or two instead.

To sum up, confronted by three bad taxes, my recommended strategy for damage limitation is to: halve the rates of the STT and recoup the revenue by increasing the rates of capital gains tax on securities transactions; abolish the BCTT; and withdraw the FBT while raising the corresponding revenue through a marginal increase in the company tax rate. Do I expect these suggestions to be implemented? Well, as the bard said, "hope springs eternal in the human breast..."

21

A curate's egg

This budget's raft of tax policy proposals is like the curate's egg, good in parts. Let's begin with the tastier morsels. First, and perhaps most important, the budget speech commits the government to phase in a national Goods and Services Tax (GST) in the four years to April 2010. If this happens, it will be a truly historic (an overworked word these days) accomplishment in India's tax reform journey. At least the government's intention has been formally proclaimed and must be warmly welcomed. The announcement's credibility quotient would have much higher if the target date had been set for April 2009, within the allotted five-year span of the present government. But let's hope for the best.

Second, the budget makes actual forward movement towards the announced medium-term objective by raising the general services tax rate from 10 to 12 per cent, in the direction of convergence with the CENVAT 16 per cent rate for goods. Third, the minister has correctly noted that, "the bane of excise and customs tariff is the plethora of exemptions." He has gone on to remove some of them. Somewhat discordantly, he has also created a few more. More importantly, he has pioneered the publication of an annual "statement on revenue foregone" or a "tax expenditure statement" as part of the budget papers. This is truly innovative and important. It's also quite an eye-opener as numerous editorials have already noted. These public estimates (and one can quibble about the methodology) can become a potent weapon in the arduous struggle to reduce tax preferences and exemptions enjoyed by various sectional interests. Finally, the budget leaves the rates of company and personal income taxes unchanged. The minister has also restrained his usual proclivity for introducing controversial new taxes, at least as far as direct taxes are concerned.

That pretty much completes the delectable parts of the curate's egg (literary types may google to refer to George du Maurier's cartoon in *Punch* of November 9, 1895). The rest of the tax policy meal is forgettably bad. To begin with, I find it quite depressing that well into the first decade of the 21st century, when simple folk are glibly chatting about fast-breeder reactors, comprehension of the budget's tax proposals still requires a solid background in inorganic chemistry. Alright, PVC is almost a household word. But LDPE, PP, EDC, VCM DMT, PTA, MEG? I ask you! All this is eloquent testimony to the utterly needless (and dysfunctional) complexity of our indirect tax structure. It takes the minister a full 37 paragraphs to merely 'outline' his indirect tax proposals. Incredible India, indeed! In contrast, in most modern tax structures annual indirect tax proposals are confined to minor changes in the general VAT rate and a couple of customs duties.

Turning to customs, this was a golden opportunity to converge all non-agricultural rates to just two, 10 and 5 per cent (even a single rate of 10 might have been possible). This would have been especially easy when a fresh 4 per cent CVD was being levied. (By the way, how come all the pink papers pounced on poor Yashwant Sinha for his 4 per cent SAD in 1998, while there is hardly a peep of protest from them now when Chidambaram repeats a similar measure? Perhaps, they are distracted by fast breeders…). No such luck. Instead we are treated to a measly 2.5 per cent reduction in the peak rate down to 12.5 per cent and a promiscuous proliferation in other rates—2, 5, 7.5, 10, entailing an impressive variety of effective protection rates (of value added). Obviously, simplicity and economic logic are no match for the persuasive powers of established industrial interests.

The budget's excise proposals are even less palatable. After a *pro forma* genuflection towards "our intention to converge all rates at the CENVAT rate" the speech goes on to outline a bewildering variety of 'new' concessions and deviations from the 16 per cent CENVAT for goods such as packaged foods, footwear, DVD drives, LPG stoves, lamps and synthetic yarns and fibres. For footwear alone we now have three rates of excise: zero, 8 per cent and 16 per cent! In effect, the concessional rates of 12 and 8 per cent, originally intended for exceptional items, are becoming increasingly populated. And the number of exempted products has increased.

Such multiplicity of rates makes for bad tax policy for several reasons. First, it strengthens the incentives for the general run of producers to seek concessional rates and thereby, undermines the integrity of the 16 per cent CENVAT rate. Second, the prevalence of multiple rates means that commodities in a production chain suffer value-added taxation at varied (and often unpredictable) rates. (In contrast, if all goods were taxed at 16 per cent, then value added at all stages would also bear that same rate of tax). Even the supposedly expert practitioners of this complex tax policy are often innocent of the actual results. Witness the need (in this budget) to retract the recently granted exemption for computers because domestic manufactures have woken up to the need to avail of CENVAT credit. Third, new exemptions on final products create pressure for exemptions at earlier stages in the production chain, thus playing havoc with a VAT system. Fourth, the avowed use of 'temporary' excise concessions to promote specific industries (as in the case of synthetic yarns and fibres) is totally at odds with a stable CENVAT (or GST) structure and betrays a weak understanding of a true VAT system (my more worldly friends pity my naivete, since they attribute such concessions to powerful industrial lobbies and not to any misunderstanding of the VAT system).

Regarding direct taxes, the stability of the key rates has already been commended. No such welcome can be extended to the perseverance with the two bad taxes introduced in the previous budget, namely the FBT and the cash withdrawal tax (see chapter 20). This budget has introduced another new bad 'tax' in the form of a mandated, below-market interest rate for short-term agricultural loans. This 'tax' on cooperative and commercial banks is to be compensated through subventions channelled through NABARD. Basically, it is a throwback to the bad old days of subsidised credit and interest-rate controls, which also treats banks as government departments. The poor old RBI must be squirming in discomfort.

All in all, this budget's tax policies are a very mixed bag. They could easily have been much, much better. And you can't even blame the Left.

G

Foreign trade and payments

22

Wanted: a trade policy

A week ago, the Doha Round of multilateral trade negotiations (MTN) came to a grinding halt in Cancun, Mexico. The media (domestic and foreign) is replete with the blame game (who caused the impasse: the European Union, the Americans or the G-21 of developing countries?) and the creation of new heroes and villains. Most of the Indian media has already crowned Arun Jaitley as the developing country knight in shining armour who tamed the dragons of Pascal Lamy (EU) and Bob Zoellick(US) and ensured that the virtuous stance of developing countries was not besmirched by an unfair deal in world trading arrangements. (It's another matter that, according to the *Financial Times* of London, the G-21 was led by the Brazilian Foreign Minister!). There are already many views of what exactly happened and who did what to whom. There is also plenty of mercantilist jingoism sloshing around. But its time to ask the hard questions. What does this mean for the future of world trade? What are the implications for India? Above all, what should be India's foreign trade policy in the post-Cancun world?

Amongst those who follow this stuff, a consensus is already developing about the implications of the Cancun debacle for the future of world trade. In summary, it runs as follows. The MTN train has been shunted to a siding, even if it has not been totally wrecked. Whether this is for a year, two or more, nobody really knows. The big trading powers will switch their focus and energy to the alternative tracks of preferential trading areas and bilateral deals. The US and EU have nurtured these more exclusive trading arrangements for many years under the rubric of 'open regionalism'. Now they will give them even greater importance. The US may seek to expand NAFTA into a Free Trade Area of the Americas, while maintaining a pivotal position in APEC. The world's largest economy is also likely to proliferate a whole new set of bilateral trading arrangements with individual countries, driven as much (or more) by political and foreign policy considerations as by economic rationality. The EU will concentrate on absorbing its 10 new members and prepare the ground for further expansion eastwards. The East Asian countries will, as always, be thoroughly pragmatic and eclectic, deepening existing markets in US and EU, courting China and Japan, and retooling ASEAN and APEC.

Where does this leave India? A little bit out in the cold, I am afraid—if we are not careful. We don't have any natural geographic or (recent) historic affinity with the big trading groups of the world (it's too early to call them blocs!): North America, Europe and East Asia. Nor, thanks to four decades of protectionism and one of partial liberalisation, do we attract really serious interest from these major groupings. Our own local grouping of SAPTA doesn't generate much intra-regional trade because of this region's anti-trade history and relatively low average incomes (the two tend to go together!). But that doesn't mean we have to despair. It just means we have to try harder!

So what should be our trade policy? I suggest it should encompass four elements or planks, in ascending order of importance. First, like the big trading powers, we should nurture whatever existing preferential and bilateral trading arrangements that we are already party to. This includes SAFTA, the Bangkok Agreement, the Indo-Sri Lanka Free Trade Agreement and the Indo-Nepal Trade Treaty. In terms of our total trade, the portion channelled through these preferential and bilateral arrangements doesn't amount to much and is unlikely to do so in the foreseeable future. Still, we should try and get what mileage we can from them.

Second, we should pursue, with renewed vigour, the possibilities for deepening our links with ASEAN and APEC. These trading and commercial arrangements include important trading nations, which are not too far from us geographically. Our past success in this has been limited, partly because of late-blooming interest on our part and mostly, because these (largely) East Asian countries remain uncomfortable with our inward-looking and protectionist proclivities. But if we lower our tariff and trading barriers significantly in future (along the lines announced by several Budget speeches in the last five years), then the scope for expanding mutually beneficial trading arrangements with dynamic East Asia may expand commensurately.

Third, we must be prepared to engage proactively if (and when) the Doha Round is resuscitated. Contrary to a lot of populist claptrap, WTO discipline of global trading practices and policies is at least as much (probably more) in the interests of weak trading nations (like us) as they are for the big trading powers. The latter can always deploy their political and commercial muscle to get what they want. Lacking that muscle, weaker trading nations stand to gain from global rules on world trade which apply uniformly to weak and strong trading countries. The key GATT/WTO principles of non-discrimination and most-favoured-nation treatment have been enormously beneficial whenever they have been allowed to work. If WTO principles and rules atrophy post-Cancun, we developing countries will be the big losers. Correspondingly, we should work to nudge the Doha Round back on track, while recognising that the main decisions lie largely beyond our control. This does not mean that we must accept any available deal in the MTN process. But it should mean a continuing willingness to engage constructively on most agendas.

Fourth, and by far the most important, we must reinvigorate our declared agenda of unilateral trade liberalisation. When we did this last, by reducing substantially our extremely high customs tariffs in the first half of the nineties, our foreign trade (exports and imports) grew smartly and the economy enjoyed significant gains in productivity. Our tariffs are still among the highest in the

countries. There can even be PTAs in which all parties are PTAs, such as the EC-MERCOSUR agreement under discussion.

As of 2000, the WTO identified 240 PTAs in the world! Of these, some 170 were already in force and the remainder under discussion/negotiation. In sheer number, about 90 per cent of the PTAs took the form of FTAs and only 10 per cent were customs unions. But that 10 per cent included heavy weight players like the ever expanding EC. Historically, the Euro-Mediterranean region boasted a high concentration of PTAs. In recent decades, the Americas and Asia have seen a lot of PTA activity.

What is the impact of a PTA on trade and welfare? Until the early 1950s, the presumption was that formation of a PTA was necessarily trade liberalising and therefore, resulted in freer trade and greater economic efficiency. This conventional wisdom was convincingly challenged by economists (subsequently, Nobel laureates) Jacob Viner and James Meade. They pointed out that a PTA had two kinds of effects: 'trade creation' and 'trade diversion'. Trade creation occurred when (as a result of a PTA) a country's domestic production was replaced by lower cost imports from a partner country. Trade diversion occurred when low cost imports from the rest of the world (outside the PTA) were replaced by higher cost imports from partner countries because of tariff preferences. They argued that a PTA would be welfare-enhancing, only when its trade creation effects outweighed its trade diversion effects. The conditions under which this would occur would depend on several factors. For example, if the partners to a PTA had widely different factor endowments and economic structures, then there is a much higher likelihood of trade creation gains outweighing trade diversion losses. There is a lot more to the theory of PTAs, but the Meade-Viner insight is crucial.

Economists, especially trade economists, tend to be deeply suspicious of the alleged benefits of PTAs. The Meade-Viner analysis is one reason. Another is that the discriminatory preferences built into any PTA are deeply antithetical to the principle of non-discrimination, which underpins the vision of a liberal world trading order. Then there is the whole range of problems to do with defining and policing rules of origin (ROOs) in any PTA. These have to be framed to ensure that the tariff preferences are accorded only to goods 'actually produced' in the partner countries and not to goods from the rest of the world seeking entry into the PTA through the country with the lowest external tariff. Documentation and enforcement of these ROOs can be costly (remember NAFTA had nearly 200 pages of ROOs!). Bemoaning the proliferation of PTAs, Jagdish Bhagwati has warned that, "the world trading system comes to look like a spaghetti bowl of ever-more complicated trade barriers, each depending on the supposed 'nationality' of products."

If the economic benefits of PTAs are so dubious, how come they have mushroomed in such large numbers over the last 50 years? There seem to be several reasons. First, PTAs are often driven by non-economic or extra-economic reasons. For example, the formation of the EC was heavily conditioned by the post-war drive for greater political unity in Europe. An important motivation for NAFTA was to check the flood of illegal migrant labour from Mexico to USA. Many developing country PTAs are also driven substantially by motivations of political cooperation and solidarity, such as SAPTA, MERCOSUR and ASEAN. (It may not be wholly coincidental that the primary support for many developing country PTAs comes from foreign ministries and offices of presidents and prime ministers rather than usual economic ministries). Second, many of the economic downsides of PTAs (including trade diversion costs) have been contained by the general trend of lower tariffs and trade barriers brought about through multilateral and unilateral trade liberalisation in the past half century. Third, the major trading powers (US and EC) have frequently pressed ahead on the 'dirt road' of regional trade agreements when the 'turnpike' of multilateral trade liberalisation has been temporarily blocked. More bluntly, these major trading powers have often used the carrot of PTA access to their huge markets to pry open trade barriers in other countries. All this comes under the so-called doctrine of 'open regionalism'.

So what is the lesson of all this for India's recent burst of PTA enthusiasm? I would make four points. First, the economic costs and benefits of each of the new PTAs will depend crucially on the details of the product lists, phasing, rules of origin, etc. Any sweeping judgement would be premature. Second, since Thailand and other ASEAN countries are closer to us in economic structure and resource endowments than industrialised countries, we should not expect huge trade creation gains. Those could be expected if we were to enter a FTA with US or EC. Nevertheless, since ASEAN countries are much more open economies than India, there is merit in our joining such trade-friendly clubs. Third, as I argued last month (*Business Standard*, September 23), our new found fondness for PTAs should not distract us from the more strenuous (but more rewarding) endeavour of multilateral trade liberalisation under WTO auspices. Fourth, and most importantly, we don't have to wait for any agreements with anyone to reap enormous benefits of freer trade. All we have to do is to carry through the tariff reductions promised in successive budget speeches by successive finance ministers of recent years. Of course, the gains from such unilateral trade liberalisation would be greater if we solved our infrastructure bottlenecks and other policy impediments to industrial competitiveness. These include, the 'usual suspects' such as labour laws and small-scale reservations as well as the growing problem of an appreciating rupee.

24

A common currency for SAARC?

Earlier this year, at the 12th SAARC summit held in Islamabad, then Prime Minister Vajpayee mooted the vision of a common currency for SAARC. Is this a goal worth pursuing seriously? Or is it one of those PMO/MEA 'economic initiatives' with low economic rationality and high temporary utility for fleshing out a prime ministerial speech in a regional summit? (Incidentally, it is noteworthy that last autumn's official enthusiasm for free-trade-area initiatives has subsided somewhat in the face of reality and some serious questioning by a new prime minister with full command over the economics of international trade). Irrespective of pedigree, let's evaluate the proposal on merits.

Those in favour of a common SAARC currency usually advance four main arguments in support. First, they argue that a common currency is a characteristic of strong regional economic integration and therefore, a worthy goal. Second, they point out that currency unification will eliminate exchange risk and uncertainty and thereby, promote inter-country trade and investment. Third, these objectives will also be advanced by the reduction of transaction costs arising from currency conversions. Fourth, advocates back a currency union in the belief that it will promote political unity amongst the constituent nations.

Let's consider these arguments in turn. The first argument is really not an argument at all. It simply states that regional economic integration is a good thing and therefore, we should pursue it by all available means, including a common currency. It begs the obvious question of whether such integration is in the national economic interest of the cooperating nations. That question can only be answered by exploring the costs and benefits of economic cooperation through various means. Similarly, the fourth argument is only a statement of faith, not supported by experience. In the long sweep of history, common currencies have usually followed political unification (often attained through imperial conquest). Political unity has not been catalysed through currency unification. One possible notable exception is the 50 year old enterprise of European unification, spawned by the trauma of two world wars. In this case, clearly the advent of the euro has preceded full political unity. But, even in this instance, it is far from clear whether currency unification (covering a subset of the countries of the recently expanded European Union) is promoting or impeding political unification.

Returning to South Asia, it is surely a very wishful pipe dream to think that the fault lines of political conflict and rivalry between India and Pakistan (to take the obvious bilateral pairing) can be effectively bridged through a programme of monetary unification. On the contrary, the slow progress of SAFTA suggests that political antagonisms have and will seriously impede efforts at regional economic cooperation.

The second and third arguments (of eliminated exchange risk and reduced transaction costs) are genuine economic benefits of a common currency. The question is how significant are these benefits for South Asian countries and how do they stack up against the very real costs that currency unification imposes on participating nations?

A rough guide to the significance of these purported economic benefits is provided by the importance of intra-SAARC trade in relation to the total trade of SAARC countries. This ratio has hovered in the range of only 4 to 5 per cent over the past decade, despite SAFTA and various bilateral FTAs among SAARC nations. Contrast this low number with 50 per cent plus for NAFTA and

20 per cent plus for ASEAN. (Incidentally, there isn't much impetus for a common currency in even these more successful regional trading arrangements). Furthermore, intra-SAARC cross-border flows of capital are even less significant in relation to total investment flows into SAARC nations. Therefore, as a first approximation, it is clear that the benefits from a common currency are likely to be modest for SAARC members.

What about the costs? Although regional integration enthusiasts tend to gloss over these, the costs can be quite substantial for member countries. The most obvious costs arise from the loss of sovereign control over monetary and exchange rate policies. A common currency means that these policies would be conducted by some version of a SAARC central bank which would subsume much of the policymaking prerogatives of today's national central banks of SAARC nations. To put it bluntly, the RBI (together with finance ministry) would no longer determine India's monetary and exchange rate policies. Before turning to the economic costs, we should frankly recognise that the political and psychological costs of such loss of monetary independence are likely to be very substantial for all member countries and their governments.

As for economic costs arising from the loss of policy autonomy, the literature on 'optimum currency area' indicates that such costs are likely to be higher to the extent that business cycles across member states are not synchronised and to the extent that member nations are subject to different (in time and degree) shocks, to which their economies have to adjust. The huge economic costs recently suffered by Argentina at the collapse of its unsustainable currency board system (a weaker version of a common currency with the US) should offer some warning to armchair proponents of currency union for SAARC.

Recent econometric studies by Maskay (e.g. in *South Asia Economic Journal*, 2001) and others have shown that there has been no significant synchronisation of economic cycles (as reflected in trends in GDP growth and inflation) among SAARC countries in the two decades 1980-2000. What this means is that the monetary authorities in each SAARC country had to contend with rather different business cycle conditions at any given point in time. Conversely, any uniform monetary and exchange rate policy imposed by a regional SAARC central bank would not have been in the interests of individual member countries. These studies also suggest that the pattern of exogenous political and climatic 'shocks' experienced by SAARC countries was quite diverse, despite some emerging trends of convergence in trade and exchange rate liberalisation.

Overall, the empirical studies point to substantial divergence in the pattern of business cycles and shocks across SAARC countries. This, in turn, means that SAARC countries are better-off retaining the freedom of policy action available with separate central banks and independent monetary and exchange rate policies.

None of this should come as a surprise, given the very limited degree of economic integration achieved across SAARC countries thus far. Nor is the situation likely to change dramatically in the foreseeable future.

Advocacy of a common SAARC currency at present is really a case of putting the cart before the horse. We need far freer movement of goods, services, capital and people across borders within SAARC before the issue of currency unification can be treated as serious. In any case, there is no real political appetite for a common currency. The largest SAARC country, India, would consider ceding monetary autonomy to a regional SAARC central bank, only if India effectively controlled that institution's policies. Under those conditions, the smaller SAARC nations are hardly likely to sign on for a common currency.

To sum up, there are compelling economic and political reasons against a common currency for SAARC. It's an idea whose time has not yet come…and quite possibly, never will.

25

A new BoP paradigm?

Over the past year or so, there has been a lively debate on a set of interlinked issues, including the surge in foreign capital inflows, the growing mountain of forex reserves (and how to deploy them productively) and the appropriate monetary, fiscal and exchange rate policies in response to these developments. Much of the attention has been focused on inflows from foreign institutional investors (FIIs), who invested $ 11 billion net in the Indian capital market in 2003/04 and a comparable amount in the present fiscal year as of mid-February. In much of the discussion, there has been an explicit or implicit presumption that 'foreign capital surge' is the major new phenomenon, which our macroeconomic policies are having to contend with.

In fact, is capital surge the only 'new' development in our external finances? Or even the most important one? It's time to look at a few numbers. Table 25.1 compares key elements of India's balance of payments (BoP) for the first three years after the crisis year of 1991/92 *versus* the three most recent years for which full BoP data are available. For each triennium, ratios to GDP have been computed and annual averages taken. Several trends are noteworthy.

First, the share of both exports and imports in GDP have increased, partly reflecting the rupee's depreciation over the intervening decade. Second, there has been a small increase in the merchandise trade deficit to 2.7 per cent of GDP (actually it was running even higher in the period 1995/96 to 1999/00, reaching a peak of 4 per cent in the latter year). Third, and far more significantly, the balance on 'invisibles' account has more than tripled from 1.1 per cent of GDP in the early 1990s to 3.5 per cent in the recent period. About two-thirds of this massive increase is attributable to the rapid growth of software exports from negligible levels to over $ 12 billion in 2003/04. The other third is accounted for by the continuing growth of private transfers or remittances from NRIs; these amounted to over $ 19 billion in 2003/04.

As a result of the sustained surge in 'net invisibles', India's long-standing, 'structural' deficit in the current account of the BoP has swung into surplus in recent years. This is a much more significant development than the surge in capital inflows. Indeed, comparing 2001-2004 with 1992-1995, the data don't reveal a jump in the capital account balance, even though the composition of capital flows has changed. There isn't even a pronounced rise in FII inflows, partly because the earlier period also included a temporary surge in such flows. Finally, powered by the turnaround in the current account and continued buoyancy in capital account inflows, the average rate of forex reserve accretion has quadrupled over the decade from around $ 5 billion per year in the early 1990s to about $ 20 billion per year in recent years.

We can summarise the evolution in India's BOP as follows. In the first part of the 1990s, a merchandise trade deficit of over 2 per cent of GDP was partially offset by an invisibles surplus of about half that magnitude, leaving a current account deficit of around one per cent of GDP. Set against net capital inflows in the order of 2.5 to 3 per cent of GDP, this led to an overall BOP balance (broadly equivalent to forex reserve accretion) in the range of 1.5 to 2 per cent of GDP. Over the ensuing decade, the tripling in net invisibles has transformed the picture and brought about a swing (from negative to positive) of about 2 per cent of GDP in the current account balance. With capital inflows almost constant (as a ratio to GDP), this means that the annual rate of forex reserve accretion has risen sharply to average close to 4 per cent of GDP. Thus, it is the surges in software exports and private remittances that are the main new contributors to the embarrassment of forex riches, with FII inflows playing only an amplifying role in particular years like 2003 and 2004.

What are the implications of this diagnosis for policy? At one level, the challenge posed by 'excessive' reserve accretion for macroeconomic policy remains the same, irrespective of whether the increased flows are coming from the current or capital account. The RBI's basic options continue to be three: allow the exchange rate to appreciate, augment forex reserves without 'sterilising' them (that is, without compensatory reduction of RBI's domestic assets) or add to reserves and sterilise the monetary consequences. Or, of course, some combination of these three. Of the three primary options, unsterilised intervention is generally the least preferred because of the high (and politically unacceptable) risks of accelerated inflation.

In judging the appropriate policy response, one key issue is the durability of the 'excess' flows or new trends. If the flows are temporary, then there is a strong case for buying them into reserves (without disturbing the exchange rate) and sterilising the monetary consequences. This has been the RBI's preferred response over the past three or four years. However, as everyone knows, sterilised intervention has growing fiscal costs since low return forex assets are substituted for higher earning government bonds. These fiscal penalties have to be compared with more nebulous but real costs of allowing exchange-rate appreciation, including, primarily, the reduction in international competitiveness. It could be argued that the growth of remittances and software exports in the past decade is likely to be more durable than occasional surges in FII flows. In that case the RBI's (and the government's) dilemma of choosing between rupee appreciation and fiscal costs of sterilisation acquires a sharper edge. The dilemma becomes even worse if the rise in capital inflows is also sustained.

The best resolution of the dilemma would be through an increase in the rate of investment (especially, productive private investment). Anything that government can do to improve the investment climate and thereby, trigger higher investment (relative to savings) would help move the current account in the BOP towards deficit and thereby, relieve the pressure to acquire more forex reserves. The list of investment-promoting reforms is well known. So, unfortunately, is the government's apparent incapacity to deliver on them. The import-promoting option of reducing peak import duties is more feasible and can be engineered in a revenue neutral way. Incremental enhancement of capital account convertibility is a third option, which the RBI has pursued, but it is limited by the vulnerability of the domestic fiscal situation and the financial system. Pumping up public investment is another alternative but that runs the real risk of even higher fiscal deficits and its various associated costs, including damping of private investment. An even worse option is to stoke government current expenditure and reduce public savings.

Which of these options will the government pursue? My guess is all of them, including, regrettably, the last. The only saving grace is that the more economically unsound is the mix of options, the quicker will be the reversal in the recently burgeoning FII inflows. That will lessen the RBI's forex management problem but it could also dent the current bull market and the ongoing recovery in industrial activity and investment. These are interesting times for macroeconomic management. Let's hope the government's economic policies are equal to the challenge.

Table 25.1

Balance of payments

(All entries are as per cent of GDP at current market prices)

	Average of 1992/93—1994/95	Average of 2001/02—2003/04
Exports, f.o.b.	8.0	10.0
Imports, c.i.f.	10.2	12.7
Trade balance	**-2.2**	**-2.7**
Invisibles, net	**1.1**	**3.5**
of which:		
(Private remittances)	(2.0)	(2.9)
(Software exports)	(0.1)	(1.8)
Current account balance	**-1.1**	**0.8**
Capital account balance	**2.7**	**2.9**
Of which:		
(Foreign direct investment)	(0.3)	(1.0)
(Foreign portfolio investment)	(0.9)	(0.8)
(External assistance)	(0.6)	(-0.2)
('Other capital')*	(0.7)	(1.1)
Reserves increase	**1.7**	**3.7**

Note: * Consists mainly of banking capital flows (other than NRI deposits) and 'Leads' and 'Lags' in payments and receipts for imports and exports.

Source: Reserve Bank of India.

26

Global imbalances

'Global imbalances' have become a hardy perennial on the international conference circuit for senior finance mandarins of governments and international financial institutions, as well as academic economists. For several years, a majority of both sets of attendees have issued dire warnings for the world economy if the imbalances are not moderated. Yet the world economy continues to power ahead at 5 per cent per year, while the imbalances continue to increase. What's going on? On the strength of participation in one of these international seminars on the subject (typically in salubrious locales—this one was at a Cape Cod resort in Massachusetts), let me share a few thoughts.

What's the problem of 'global imbalances'? The most prominent symptom or yardstick is the steadily increasing current account deficit in the balance of payments of the United States, which has risen from $ 114 billion (or 1.5 per cent of GDP) in 1995 to $ 805 billion (or 6.4 per cent of GDP) in 2005 and is projected to rise further in 2006. This scale of sustained and rising deficits has never before been experienced by the US (or any significant industrial nation). Just think. In 2005 the world's biggest and richest economy took in $ 800 billion of savings by the rest of the world. In the five years 2001-2005, the foreign savings absorbed was nearly 3 trillion dollars, turning the globe's single superpower into a significant debtor nation. This outcome is quite contrary to what textbooks predict (savings will flow from capital-heavy, rich countries to capital-starved, poor ones) and to the *Pax Brittanica* decades, when imperial Britain was a major net creditor channelling savings to the empire. The present, unprecedented foreign savings inflow into the US has been described as the largest programme of 'external assistance' in history, with the notable flaw that the recipient is the most powerful economy on earth!

Associated (but not congruent) with this peculiar phenomenon of capital 'flowing up the hill' is the increasingly lopsided pattern of international reserve holding. In the past four years global foreign exchange reserve holdings have increased by over 2 trillion dollars, of which China alone accounted for nearly $ 600 billion and the rest of 'emerging Asia' and Japan for about $ 400 billion each. The bulk of international reserves are held in the form of US government treasury bills and bonds with pretty low yields. Thus, poor Asian countries (and Japan and some oil exporters) are working hard to generate surpluses, which they are 'investing' in low return US government liabilities. Again, an odd outcome, to put it mildly.

Aside from being very peculiar, the recent trajectory of global finances is also fraught with serious risks. First, almost everyone recognises that the pattern of large and growing US current account deficits cannot go on forever. Sooner or later, there has to be 'adjustment', brought about through some combination of higher US savings (or lower investment), higher investment (or lower saving) outside the US and a real depreciation of the dollar *versus* other currencies (equivalently a real appreciation of non-dollar currencies). The issue is whether it will be a 'hard' or 'soft' landing for the US and the world. Very likely, the longer the unprecedented trajectory of imbalances persists, the higher the risks of a disruptive hard landing, which could be triggered by a number of factors in world financial or real markets, not to mention war or pandemics. For example, a significant rise in US inflation could induce portfolio shifts away from dollar assets by foreign holders, thereby raising US and global interest rates, causing overshooting in currency adjustments and disrupting global production and trade. Second, the continued stickiness in China's real exchange rate, despite large and rising external account surpluses and reserves, could provoke

US trade restrictions on China's imports and thus trigger a major trade war to the detriment of all.

A more sanguine view of these imbalances is offered by some reputable economists (like Richard Cooper of Harvard), who focus on the surplus side of the imbalances. They emphasise that the US current account deficit has to be matched by surpluses elsewhere (barring an irritating statistical discrepancy). They note that in 2005, Japan and China each ran current account surpluses of about $ 160 billion, while oil exporters accounted for about $ 350 billion. Although the Euro area was close to balance, Germany plus neighbouring Switzerland and Netherlands boasted a surplus of $ 200 billion. These surpluses were driven by a combination of factors, including high oil prices, the tendency for high savings in ageing societies (Japan and 'Germany plus'), mercantilist trade policy (China) and relatively weak domestic systems for financial intermediation (China, Japan and oil exporters). In this view, the surpluses are the driving force behind global imbalances (remember Ben Bernanke's "savings glut"?). Moreover, the surpluses could persist (if not grow) for a few more years, after which market forces will bring about a 'soft landing' adjustment.

Well, may be. But I recall Larry Summers' warning in his L.K. Jha memorial lecture earlier this year: "the moment of maximum risk comes precisely when those concerned about sustainability lose confidence in their views as their warnings prove to have been premature and when rationalizations come to the forefront." To me, there seems to be both merit and safety in the more mainstream advocacy of a set of policies which look sensible (in themselves) for key country groupings and which 'also' gradually reduce global imbalances. What are these policies? First is a reduction in the US budget deficit, which would improve US macro balances and help reduce the current account deficit. Second is a shift in favour of domestic demand (and away from exports) in China brought about by some combination of an appreciation of the renminbi and higher domestic consumption. Third is the standard IMF recommendation for structural reforms in Europe, which would stimulate higher investment, growth and external deficits. Fourth is a range of energy policies to encourage higher conservation and faster development of non-oil substitutes. Last is a call for policies to strengthen systems of financial intermediation in all major countries (outside the US) and especially in the 'structural surplus' countries, so that more of national savings 'gluts' are productively deployed within national boundaries.

Figure 26.1

US current account deficit

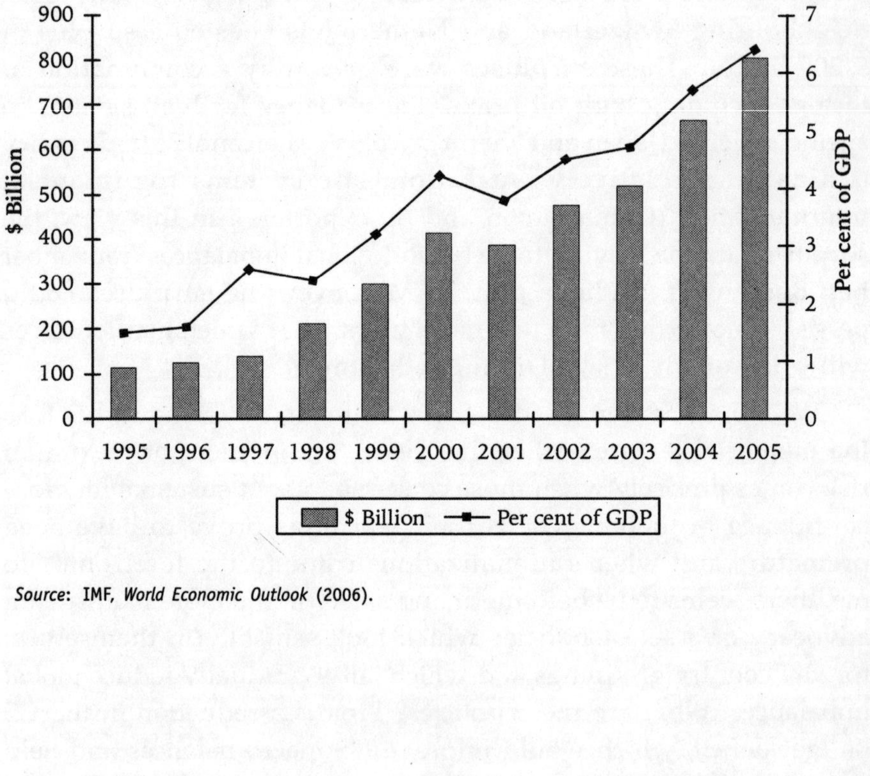

Source: IMF, *World Economic Outlook* (2006).

H

Monetary and fiscal policies

27

Inflation and monetary policy

After several years, inflation has again reared its ugly head in India. In the last four months, the annual rate of inflation (as measured by the wholesale price index or WPI) has risen from 4.5 per cent in April to 8.1 per cent in August. In response, the government has taken a number of steps including reductions in import duties on oil and steel products, commodities in which price increases has been sharpest. A fortnight ago, the Reserve Bank moved (some would say, at last) to announce an increase in the cash reserve ratio (CRR) by half a per cent to 5 per cent. There are many issues. The question I want to focus on here, is the role of monetary policy in dealing with inflation. What can we learn from our past experience? Has lax monetary policy been a significant factor behind price increases? Looking ahead, has the RBI done enough to damp the present surge in prices?

First, let's quickly review the basic facts of inflation in India. Part (a) of the Figure 27.1 shows the profile of annual inflation over the last 20 years according to three separate indices: the WPI, the CPI (for industrial workers) and the WPI for manufactures, which account for over 60 per cent weight in the overall WPI. One reason for separately tracking this last index is that it is a crude proxy for 'core' or 'underlying' inflation, which abstracts from the volatility in primary product prices and fuel prices. A glance at the figure reveals some brute facts. First, according to all three indices, inflation averaged in the band 6-8 per cent in the second half of the 1980s. Second, inflation hit double digits during the economic crisis of 1990-1992, as a result of drought, decline in industrial production and a severe import squeeze. As the economy recovered from these supply shocks and reforms kicked in, inflation moderated to around 8 per cent in 1993/94. Third, there was a rebound to double digits in 1994/95, largely because of the foreign capital surge of 1994, which resulted from the reform-induced turnaround in external sector finances. This temporary capital surge fuelled money supply growth in excess of 20 per cent. As the forex surge levelled off, so did monetary growth and inflation, though the CPI rate subsided more slowly. Fourth, after 1996, inflation (according to all indices) hovered around a 4 per cent annual rate until 2003, except for a sharp spike in the CPI in 1998/99 (the short-lived 'onion-potato inflation') and a milder uptick in the WPI in 2000/01 because of a weak monsoon and fuel price increases. It is noteworthy that 'core inflation' was mostly below 4 per cent until the uptick in 2003/04.

Part (b) of the Figure 27.1 shows recent trends in the WPI and CPI. It shows cycles around a mildly rising trend, with an upswing in WPI inflation after April 2004, one not yet reflected in the CPI.

How did monetary policy contend with earlier bouts of inflation? It played a limited role in the stabilisation programme of 1991/92; devaluation, fiscal consolidation and structural reforms took the front seats. Monetary policy was much more active in 1993-1995, when foreign exchange reserves were surging, industry was booming and inflation was rebounding. Policy had to contend with the competing pulls of accelerating industrial growth and resurgent inflation. The CRR was hiked by one per cent in summer 1994 and RBI continued with substantial sales of government securities to partially sterilise the reserve accretions. But the monetary brakes were insufficient to keep inflation from hitting 12 per cent in 1994/95, although it subsided quickly thereafter to an annual rate (point-to-point) of 8 per cent by June 1995 and below 5 per cent by March 1996. On the other hand, the economy grew at above 7 per cent for three successive years (1994-1997) and industry at double digit rates. Arguably, stronger monetary curbs may have speeded reduction in inflation but at the cost of slower growth.

Although temporary monetary squeezes were an integral part of the arsenal deployed successfully to combat contagion effects of the East Asian financial crisis and the Russian debt default in during 1997/98, inflation was not a problem. Not at least till the summer of 1998, when prices of onions and potatoes sky-rocketed by over 300 per cent! By November 1998, the CPI annual rate of inflation exceeded 20 per cent and its food component over 25 per cent. Despite extreme political discomfort from these massive price increases and pressure to undertake corrective action, the RBI (and government) correctly diagnosed the supply-shock driven price rise as temporary and largely self-correcting. Accordingly, it refrained from monetary tightening in an environment of slack investment and industrial production.

A similar tactic was followed when crude-oil prices tripled from $ 10 per barrel at the beginning of 1999 to over $ 30 in late 2000. In the space of one year, the BJP-centred coalition government(s) increased POL prices in October 1999, March 2000 and September 2000, including increases in kerosene on two occasions. Interestingly, aided by moderate money supply growth in 1999/00 and 2000/01, these commodity price increases did not lead to any lasting increase in the CPI or core inflation and only a mild and temporary rise in WPI inflation in 2000/01. The implicit lesson appeared to be that sizable commodity price shocks could be absorbed without generalised inflation, provided monetary conditions were not too lax.

After 2000/01, the main threat to low inflation has come from the massive surge in forex reserves which rose by $ 70 billion in three short years. Despite the loose fiscal policy of the government, RBI coped admirably with this unprecedented reserves build-up by undertaking large and sustained sales of government securities to offset (sterilise) the foreign assets build up. Monetary growth was contained (without sharp increases in real interest rates) and inflation remained low, helped by the combination of low world inflation and a sustained trend of trade liberalisation by India.

Inflation control was certainly helped by slack industrial demand for bank credit and the seemingly insatiable appetite of banks for government paper ('lazy banking').

So what lessons can we draw for this capsule review? First, monetary policy may not always be the magic bullet to slay the inflation dragon. Second, nevertheless, monetary policy matters. Third, supply price shocks need not result in general inflation, provided monetary and fiscal policies are not overly accommodating. Fourth, monetary damping of inflationary fires is easier when the private sector is not booming.

Returning to the present and with the benefit of 20/20 hindsight, there does seem to be a case for RBI to have signalled a mild tightening of monetary policy a few months earlier than it has chosen to do, given the uptrend in both WPI and core inflation in 2003/04 and the reversal of monetary policy stance in most major industrial economies some months ago. Still, better a little late than never (and realistically, six months ago was election season, when the central bank had to tread carefully). What is perhaps more intriguing, are recent official statements promising no upward change in interest rates. How can modern monetary policy operate on the quantity of money without affecting its price? Or is the recent CRR change purely cosmetic?

Figure 27.1

Annual inflation rates

(a) 1984/85-2003/04

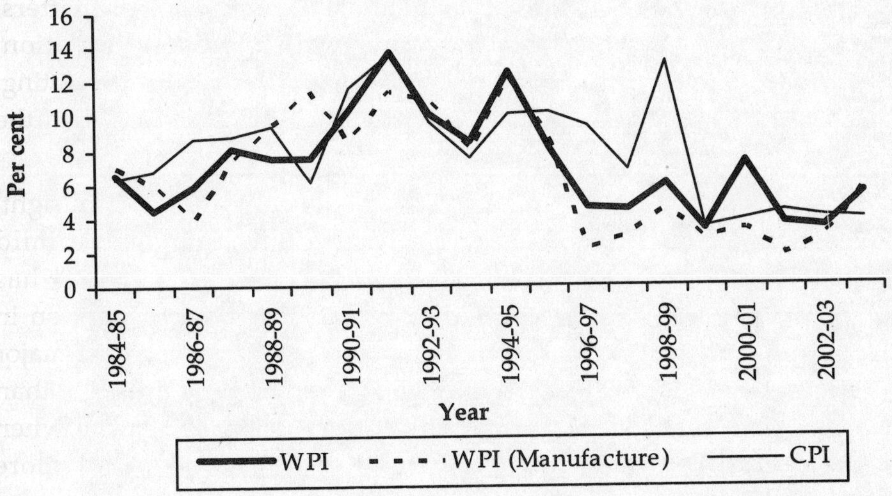

(b) *Recent trends*

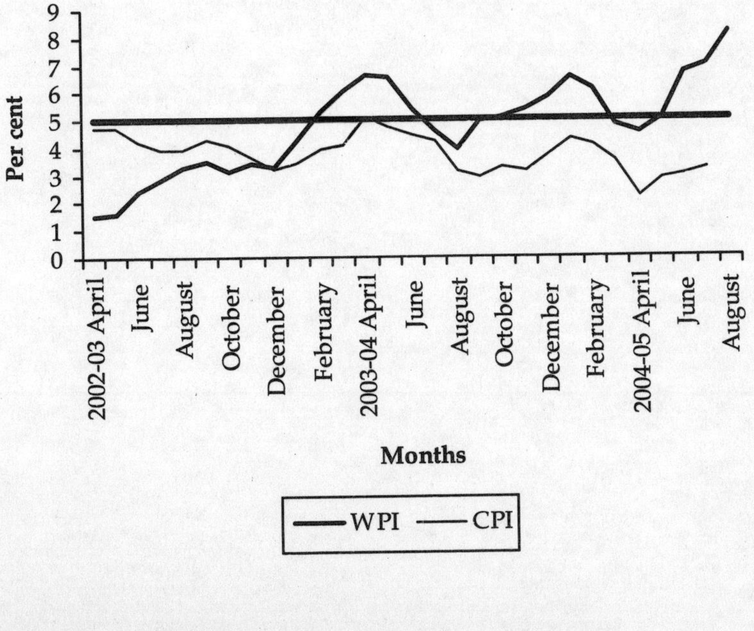

28

Farewell fiscal responsibility?

After three years of debate, Parliament passed the Fiscal Responsibility and Budget Management (FRBM) Bill into law in 2003, during the tenure of the NDA government. The law became operational with the notification of the Act and statutory Rules by the UPA government in July 2004. At that time, Finance Minister P. Chidambaram also successfully moved an amendment to the Act to relax (postpone) by one year to 2008/09 the target year by which the centre's revenue deficit had to be eliminated. The FRBM law requires, amongst other benchmarks, a minimum reduction of the revenue deficit by 0.5 per cent of GDP and of the fiscal deficit by 0.3 per cent in each year up to 2008/09. Scarcely eight months after the notification of the Act, Mr. Chidambaram in his second UPA budget has pressed the 'pause button' on the FRBM Act. He has justified this early recourse to 'pause' by pointing to the additional 'burden' of centre-state transfers entailed by the government's acceptance of the Twelfth Finance Commission (TFC) recommendations.

This brief history of the FRBM Act raises some important issues. Does this early weakening of the FRBM law in two successive budgets seriously weaken the underlying objectives of the Act? Were the TFC recommendations adequate justification for hitting the pause button on FRBM? Are even the weakened ('paused') fiscal targets in Budget 2005/06 achievable? If fiscal consolidation has been shelved, does it really matter? Let's explore these issues.

The basic purpose of the FRBM Act was to help bring about a long overdue reduction in the central government's revenue and fiscal deficits and outstanding liabilities. The logic of this kind of law is to establish an 'external' restraint on the government of the day, as it struggles to contain expenditures and raise revenues. The theory is that when Parliament has solemnly committed itself to a programme of medium-term fiscal consolidation, finance ministers making annual budgets can draw strength from the FRBM Act to beat off the perennial and vociferous demands for additional expenditure and tax reliefs. He can point to the FRBM benchmarks and say, "Look, I would have liked to provide more money for education (or rural development...or any other worthy expenditure), but I can't without breaching the FRBM targets." However, if in the first year of the new law, the benchmarks are twice relaxed in two successive budgets, then the purpose of the Act is largely defeated. The UPA and Mr. Chidambaram have clearly preferred to amend the law to accommodate the exigencies of annual budget-making, rather than the other way round. But then, why have the law if its restraints are so readily loosened?

Actually, the damage to the cause of fiscal consolidation goes beyond the central government. In recent years, the states have also been encouraged to pass similar laws to help repair their parlous finances. By endorsing TFC recommendations to make debt relief to states conditional on such enactments, the UPA government has reiterated this advice to states. But the centre's actions contradict such advice and actions speak louder than words. The obvious lesson for the states is to pass the laws (necessary to qualify for debt relief) and then amend them at will!

But what about the 'additional' Rs. 26,000 crores of TFC-recommended transfers to the states in the form of tax devolution, grants and debt relief? Doesn't that provide 'just cause' to pause FRBM targets? Not if you think about it a bit. First, the estimate of Rs. 26,000 crores seems exaggerated on several counts, including the fact that the TFC-recommended increase in the tax devolution ratio from 29.5 to 30.5 per cent has been largely negated by this budget's greater reliance on surcharges and cesses, 'which are not shared with states'. Second, in a budget of more than Rs. 500,000 crore, it is surely a trifle unreasonable to single out one item of additional expenditure to justify a legal amendment. What about the 'additional' Rs. 25,000 crore provided for "priority and flagship programmes falling under the NCMP"? Why not make that the culprit for FRBM amendment?

More importantly, TFC recommendations (as interpreted by Mr. Chidambaram) actually 'save' the centre's fiscal deficit Rs. 3,000 crore! How so? Well, against the Rs. 26,000 crore noted above, has to be weighed the Rs. 29,003 crore of central loan assistance to state plans, which has now been shunted from the centre's budget to states to seek directly from market, apparently "in accordance with the recommendations of the TFC." (The last bit is not strictly correct, since the TFC recommended this shift be 'phased' in 'over time'. It rightly foresaw problems with an overnight shift in financing pattern; more on this later).

Even the weak ('paused') deficit targets in the 2005/06 Budget look unattainable. More than most budgets this one suffers from optimistic revenue targets and a certain coyness in stating expenditures transparently. Consider the following. Personal income tax revenues are projected to grow by 30 per cent despite sizable reductions in real tax rates at all income levels, engineered through widened tax brackets. Last time (1997/98) Mr. Chidambaram reduced tax rates, income tax revenues fell by 6 per cent. So, achieving even 10 per cent growth may not be easy. A shortfall of around Rs. 10,000 crore on this item seems a safe bet. Similarly, excise revenues are expected to increase by 21 per cent, when the historical record justifies only 10 to 11 per cent (Table 28.1). Another Rs. 10,000 crore of likely shortfall here. Company taxes are projected to grow by 33 per cent on top of last year's 31 per cent and against a historical average closer to 20 per cent. I anticipate a shortfall of about Rs. 6,000 crore. Allowing for sharing with states, the centre's budget estimates for net tax revenue could be undershot by Rs. 20,000 crore.

Turning to expenditure, it is most unlikely that all the Rs. 29,003 crore of plan assistance shifted to the states for direct borrowing, will actually be raised successfully from the market at reasonable rates. Instead, many states will come knocking at the centre's door to make up the balance. A reasonable guess is that the centre will have to extend loans for about half the amount (say, Rs. 15,000 crore). Similarly, perhaps half the indicated Rs. 10,000 crore for the infrastructure special purpose vehicle will end up as budget expenditure. Possibly, there could be offsetting saving on plan expenditure of that order. So, taking revenues and expenditure together, the fiscal deficit could be overshot by about Rs. 35,000 crore (say,1 per cent of GDP) and the revenue deficit by Rs. 17,000 crore (say, 0.5 per cent of GDP). If these guesstimates transpire, Budget 2005/06 will have hit the 'reverse' button on fiscal correction quite hard! And just compare these estimates for deficits with those that Mr. Chidambaram presented in his "Medium Term Fiscal Policy Statement" in July 2004 (Table 28.2). The possibility of reducing a 3 per cent of GDP revenue deficit to zero in three years is remote. Farewell to fiscal responsibility?

So what's a little fiscal irresponsibility between friends? Especially, when the world economy is steaming ahead and dollars are pouring into India as global funds diversify into non-dollar equities. Exactly. The going is good right now and India's economy is likely to grow at 7 per cent in 2005/06. But the global tide will turn one day. When it does, there could be a nasty reckoning for India's current fiscal profligacy. As the budget speech solemnly intones, "The current phase of high growth provides us an opportunity that should not be frittered away. We must use this opportunity to improve the fiscal health of the country."

Alas, the actual budget promises less of improvement and more of frittering.

Table 28.1

Growth rates (%) of major central taxes

	Last 10 years 1995/96–2004/05	*Last 5-years 2000/01–2004/05*	*2003/04*	*2004/05 (RE)*	*2005/06 (BE)*	*2005/06 (BE) (in Rs. Crore)*
Union excise duties	10.5	10.3	10.3	11.0	20.7	121533
Customs	8.6	3.7	8.4	15.7	-5.5	53182
Corporation tax	20.1	22.6	37.7	30.6	33.2	110573
Income tax	16.1	15.0	12.3	23.1	30.1	66239

Source: Budget documents and *Economic Surveys.*

Table 28.2

Centre's fiscal and revenue deficits (per cent of GDP)

	2003/04	*2004/05 (RE)*	*2005/06*		
			MTFP Projection[a]	*BE*	*Likely*[b]
Revenue deficit	3.6	2.7	1.8	2.7	3.2
Fiscal deficit	4.5	4.5	4.0	4.3	5.3

Note: a. As projected in July 2004 Medium Term Fiscal Policy (MTFP) Statement by Finance Minister.
b. As feared by author.

29

Fiscal deficit, what's that?

As we bask in the glow of a fourth consecutive year of 8 per cent growth, we seem to have forgotten one of the perennial bugbears of the 1990s, the dreaded 'fiscal deficit'. Most economists accorded an important role to the high fiscal deficits of the late 1980s in causing the economic crisis of 1991. We spent much of the first half of the nineties decade striving, with partial success, to reduce the fiscal deficit. The second half was spent struggling, unsuccessfully, to contain the fiscal deficit from ballooning in the wake of the Fifth Pay Commission decisions. Several years of effort yielded the Fiscal Responsibility and Budget Management (FRBM) Act of 2003 (notified in 2004) at the central government level and many states have followed with similar laws (nudged along by some crucial conditionalities in the Twelfth Finance Commission's recommendations for debt relief). But today, 'the fiscal deficit' is a guaranteed conversation killer. Is that really justified? Have matters improved so much? Or has our dynamic economy matured beyond such mundane 'accountant's concerns'?

Well, let's start with a few numbers. As the table 29.1 shows, there was a significant improvement in the consolidated (centre and states) fiscal deficit from an 8.9 per cent of GDP average in 1988-1991 (it was an even higher 9.4 per cent in 1990/91) down to 6.5 per cent in 1995/96. Then, as the Fifth Pay Commission decisions took hold and the tax revenue effort weakened, the overall deficit climbed back up to nearly 10 per cent of GDP by 2001/02. Subsequently, helped by fiscal responsibility laws and better revenue performance, the deficit has been brought down to 7.5 per cent of GDP in the two most recent years. So, in the last 15 years, approximately spanning three five-year-plan periods, there has been a cycle in the fiscal deficit: down from a high level, then back up even higher and then down again.

It is interesting to note the inverse correlation between the fall-rise-fall of the fiscal deficit and the growth performance of the Indian economy during this period: strong growth of 6.7 per cent in the Eighth Plan (1992-1997) when the deficit was shrinking; some deceleration in the Ninth Plan (1997-2002) when the deficit was widening; and resurgent growth in the Tenth Plan (2002-2007) with the fiscal deficit again reducing. This inverse correlation is not wholly accidental. There may be some causality at work, operating through the usual transmission mechanisms of credit availability, real interest rates, savings and investment. (I don't wish to suggest that the variation in fiscal deficit levels is the sole factor explaining changes in GDP growth outcomes; obviously, other factors were also at work).

The numbers do suggest that the reduction in the fiscal deficit in the first half of the 1990s helped to accommodate the upsurge in private corporate savings and investment of the period, just as the subsequent widening of the fiscal and revenue deficits in the latter half of the decade contributed to a significant drop in aggregate savings and investment, especially in public savings. The latest rebound in gross investment (to 30 per cent of GDP by 2004/05) has been greatly helped by the 4 percentage point positive swing in public savings, largely attributable to the substantial drop in public dissavings brought about by the large reduction in the consolidated revenue deficit (from 7 per cent in 2001/02 to 3.7 per cent in 2004/05).

To me, the lesson in these numbers is fairly clear: fiscal (and revenue) deficits matter. We forget this at our peril. It is also a trifle disquieting to note that, after the latest round of fiscal consolidation, our fiscal position is still somewhat weaker than it was a decade ago. Today's (2005/06) fiscal deficit of 7.5 per cent of GDP is a little higher than the 6.5 in 1995/96. Actually, the gap is perhaps 0.6 per cent greater once we adjust upwards the fiscal deficit in 2005/06 by the Rs. 17,000 crores of oil bonds issued off-budget in 2005/06, as we should. (By the way, an 8 per cent fiscal deficit makes us one of the highest deficit countries in the world). Furthermore, the government debt to GDP ratio at 83 per cent in March 2006 is a good deal worse than the 63 per cent in March 1996. The vulnerability to increases in interest rates is obvious.

What's the fiscal outlook for the future? Mixed, at best. On the positive side are the recently enacted fiscal responsibility laws at the central and state levels. But we know from the central government's example in 2005/06 that such legislated trajectories can be 'paused' when the government finds the restraints too inconvenient. Nor does it help to have the Planning Commission and Left parties advocating further 'pauses' in the Eleventh Plan. The other positive feature of the fiscal outlook is the buoyancy in state government revenue associated with the switch to VAT systems of sales taxation in the last couple of years. This could yield further returns as organised retail trade gathers steam. So could the implementation of a well-designed system for national Goods and Services Tax (GST) as recommended by the Kelkar Task Force in 2004, which was announced for implementation in this year's budget speech. But the target date was put disappointingly distant (April 2010) and there are not many signs of serious preparatory work.

On the negative side, there are at least three major threats to fiscal consolidation in the medium term. First, the tax exemptions built into the Special Economic Zones scheme are unduly generous and could seriously erode the revenue base in the medium-term. Second, the populist programmes (such as the national rural employment guarantee scheme) of the UPA government pose serious budgetary headaches for the future (see *Business Standard*, December 27, 2005). Perhaps most important is the possible fall out from the Sixth Pay Commission, which is expected to present its report in late 2008. If it is similar to the consequences of the predecessor commission, then we are in for a very rough ride on the fiscal front.

The bottom line is that if we don't take the fiscal deficit seriously (as we patently don't today), then it could easily widen and harm our future growth and development. It's done it before, it can do so again.

Table 29.1

Deficits, savings and investment (% of GDP at current market prices)

	1988-1991 (Avg)	*1995/96*	*2001/02*	*2004/05*	*2005/06 RE*
1. Gross fiscal deficit (Consolidated)	**8.9**	**6.5**	**9.9**	**7.5**	**7.5**
2. Gross primary deficit (Consolidated)	**4.8**	**1.6**	**3.7**	**1.4**	**1.6**
3. Gross revenue deficit (Consolidated)	**3.4**	**3.2**	**7.0**	**3.7**	**3.1**
4. Gross domestic savings	**22.1**	**25.1**	**23.6**	**29.1**	**NA**
a) Household sector	18.1	18.2	22.0	22.0	NA
b) Private corporate	2.4	4.9	3.6	4.8	NA
c) Public sector	1.6	2.0	-2.0	2.2	
(of which Govt.)	(-2.2)	(-2.0)	(-6.0)	(-2.7)	NA
5. Net capital inflow	**2.9**	**1.8**	**-0.6**	**1.0**	**1.3**
6. Gross domestic investment	**25.0**	**26.9**	**23.0**	**30.1**	**NA**

Average growth rate (%)

	Eighth Plan (1992-1997)	*Ninth Plan (1997-2002)*	*Tenth Plan (2002-2007)*
GDP	6.7	5.5	7.2*
GDP per capita	4.6	3.6	5.5*

Note: * Assuming GDP growth in 2006/07 is 8 per cent as projected by RBI in October 2006.

Source: RBI, *Handbook of Statistics on the Indian Economy, 2005/06* and CSO website.

I

Foreign affairs

30

Not in China's league

Over the past few months, there have been a number of articles in international magazines and newspapers extolling the rise of China and India in the world economy. Phrases like "the two Asian giants" have become commonplace. More fanciful commentators have concocted new terms like "Chindia" to herald the rise of this new global force. Futurologists have speculated about a 'tripolar' scenario of the US, China and India, dominating global affairs in decade or two from now. All this has stroked our fragile Indian egos no end. It may even have fooled a lot of people into actually believing all this hyperbole. It's time for a cold dash of reality and a few comparative numbers.

Let's first acknowledge the germs of truth behind the hoopla. Yes, China and India are the only two countries with populations of a billion plus. Yes, both countries have clocked strong economic growth since 1980, China at a spectacular 9 per cent plus and India at nearly 6 per cent. Yes, both countries have opened up to international trade and capital in the past quarter of a century, decisively in China and more hesitantly in India. Yes, if present growth rates are sustained, China will rival the US economy (measured at internationally comparable (PPP) prices) by 2020 and India could be the next largest economy, though trailing far behind. And yes, respected scholars estimate that in the 1950s India's per capita GNP was significantly higher than China's.

But that was back then. After the sweeping economic reforms of the late 1970s, the Chinese economic juggernaut picked up astonishing momentum, which it has sustained over the past quarter of a century through brilliant, determined and pragmatic policies. Per capita GDP growth has averaged 8 per cent in the 25 years since 1980, more than double the quickening growth rate of Indian per capita GDP. Somewhere between 1975 and 1985, Chinese average income is believed to have surpassed India's. Since then, it has kept forging ahead. By 2003 China's per capita GNP was at least 70 per cent higher than India's and her economy was more than twice as large as India's. Much of China's growth was powered by labour-intensive manufactured exports, which took the share of manufacturing in GDP to nearly 40 per cent compared to a paltry 16 per cent in India.

Other indicators of living standards were just as decisively in China's favour by the turn of the millennium. China's poverty ratio (as estimated by the World Bank's dollar-a-day income criterion) was less than half India's 35 per cent. Female adult literacy was nearly double India's pathetic 45 per cent. Life expectancy in China was a solid 8 years higher that in India. Perhaps most telling, the rate of malnutrition in children under 5 years in China was only about a quarter of the shamefully high 46 per cent level in India.

If you think of infrastructure as providing the essential sinews of current and future economic development, China's lead is even more striking. Electricity production in China is nearly three times higher than in India. Tonne-kilometres of freight hauled on railways is about 4.5 times greater. Air-freight tonne-kilometres flown in China is nearly 10 times higher. Container traffic shipped through ports is an astonishing 16 times more in China (admittedly, inclusive of Hong Kong's shipping prowess). In India, we take great pride in the telecom 'revolution' of the past decade. Despite that, in 2003 the number of landlines and mobiles in India was only one-sixth the number in China.

There are still a few sceptics who question Chinese statistics. The one area where such doubts are most difficult to sustain is the external sector, where the presence of partner country data provides good checks. Here too China's dominance over India is remarkable. In 2004-05 our economic spokesmen expressed satisfaction over 80 billion dollars of merchandise exports. But this figure pales in comparison with the nearly 600 billion dollars of Chinese goods exports in 2004, which generated many millions of good jobs for Chinese workers and swamped retail outlets worldwide, to the delight of consumers and the consternation of local producers. Many of the exporting factories continued to be financed by foreign direct investment, which poured in at a rate more than 10 times higher than into India. The tourist trade was equally impressive, clocking some 33 million arrivals (exclusive of Hong Kong) compared to less than 3 million into India. Not surprisingly, in 2004, China's foreign exchange reserves were more than 4.5 times greater than India's and climbing fast.

Indeed, if one looks at the large multiples by which China's infrastructure and external indicators exceed India's, it is hard to understand why China's per capita GNP is only 1.7 greater than India's. Perhaps it has something to do with the fact that PPP price 'corrections' are much higher in the non-traded services sectors than in traded sectors of agriculture and manufacturing. And services account for well over 50 per cent of India's GDP and only a third of China's. Thus, possibly, in the purchasing power parity methodology for arriving at internationally comparable prices, India's larger services share 'enjoys' greater upward price adjustments relative to China's, thus damping the disparity in GNP (total or per capita) actually existing between the two countries.

Looking to the future, it is easier to foresee a widening of the existing economic disparities between China and India than a reduction. Just consider that in the decade between 1992 and 2002, China increased her railway freight traffic by an amount greater than India's total rail freight in 2002. Even more remarkable, the increase in China's merchandise exports in each of the last three years was greater than total Indian exports for that year! At a more qualitative level, you have only to compare the hundreds of cranes deployed in adding to the thousands of gleaming skyscrapers in Shanghai with the handful dotting Mumbai's skyline. During the last five years while we have debated the new Bangalore airport, China has built quite a few new ones! Finally, how can we hope to close the economic gap with China when almost every second Indian child is malnourished?

Let me put this bluntly: as an economy, we are simply not in China's league.

Table 30.1

China versus India

	Units	*Year*	*China*	*India*	*Ratio of China to India*
Economy/scale					
Population	millions	2003	1288	1064	1.2
GDP (PPP)	$ billion	2003	6090	2908	2.1
Per capita GDP growth	%	1980-2004	8.2	3.7	2.2
Share of manufacturing in GDP	%	2003	39	16	2.4
Living standards					
Per capita GNP (PPP)	$	2003	4980	2880	1.7
Life expectancy	years	2003	71	63	1.1
Female adult literacy	%	2002	87	45	1.9
Under 5 mortality	(per 1000)	2003	37	87	0.4
Under 5 malnutrition	%	1995-2003	12.1	45.8	0.3
Poverty ratio (% below $ a day)		2001 and 2000	16.6	34.7	0.5
Infrastructure					
Electricity production	billion kwh	2002	1640.5	596.5	2.7
Goods hauled (railways)	tonne-km billions	2002	1508.7	333.2	4.5
Container traffic (ports)	millions	2003	61.62	3.9	15.7
Air freight	tonne-km millions	2003	5650.6	580.0	9.7
Telephones (land + mobile)	(per 1000)	2003	424	71	6.0
External sector					
Merchandise exports	$ billion	2004	593.4	80.8	7.3
Service exports	$ billion	2004	62.4	51.3	1.2
Foreign direct investment (inflow)	$ billion	2004	60.6	5.5	11.0
Tourists (arrivals)	millions	2003	33.0	2.4	13.8
Foreign exchange reserves	$ billion	2004	614.5	135.2	4.5

Sources: *World Development Indicators* (2005), Institute of International Finance, RBI and CSO. 2004 data for India refer to fiscal year 2004/05.

31

China's India strategy

The following is a fictitious, recent conversation with China's master strategist (MS) in his twilight years:

SA: Thank you for agreeing to see me again, especially with your failing health. You have advised the Chinese leadership on strategy towards India for more than 50 years. What's your assessment of that strategy?

MS: Well, the strategy was good but it has worked out even better than I expected, thanks to a lot of unwitting help from your countrymen, especially the politico-administrative leadership.

SA: How so? What was the strategy? And how did we help you 'unwittingly'?

MS: Well, I will need a little time to explain. And please don't interrupt...you Indians are very bad at listening. Your incessant chatter gets in the way of your thinking. It causes confusion. I shouldn't complain...your strategic confusion has helped us a lot over the last five decades.

Way back in the mid-1950s, in the years of "Hindi-Chini bhai-bhai", I advised Mao and Zhou that in the long run India was the only serious potential challenger to China's inevitable hegemony over Asia...and perhaps the world. Therefore, we had to work to keep India weak. I had some difficulty getting their attention. They were so preoccupied with America's aggressive containment policy and our early frictions with the Soviet Union. But they listened and understood and by the late 1950s our strategy was in place. Zhou sweet-talked Nehru, while we built an all-weather strategic road across the Aksai Chin, moved our forces into Tibet and reinforced our positions along the McMahon line. Your Mr. Nehru was a good man, but he was too soft and a poor judge of people. Look how much he trusted Krishna Menon. Anyway, Nehru was no match for Mao and Zhou.

At first, we hadn't planned on a war with India. But Menon's stupid 'forward policy' gave us too good an opportunity in 1962. Through that sharp, short border conflict we achieved many things: we won a decisive military victory (a rout really) and demoralised the Indian army; we showed the world, especially Asian countries, who was the real power in Asia; we derailed your Third 5-Year Plan and sapped the momentum of your economic development; and we tightened our stranglehold on Tibet. With our unilateral ceasefire and withdrawal in the north-east, we demonstrated our maturity in global affairs.

Right from the late 1950s, we cultivated Pakistan with economic and military assistance and ensured continuous pressure on India's western borders. Our goal was to tie India down in a low-level equilibrium of incipient and debilitating conflict with Pakistan. It was quite an effective strategy and we successfully co-opted the Americans, especially Nixon-Kissinger. But then Yahya Khan and Bhutto blundered and presented Indira Gandhi with a golden chance to dismember Pakistan and help create Bangladesh. She was one tough lady, with rare strategic and tactical sense. I tell you, she was the only 'man' in your cabinet. She made a huge mistake though, in freeing 90,000 Pak POWs, without securing final agreement on the Kashmir ceasefire line as the international border, in exchange. That allowed us to continue playing the 'Pakistan card' for containing India, including through transfer of nuclear and missile technology. And, contrary to our expectations, she failed to follow through with weaponisation after showing great courage and initiative with Pokhran I.

Fortunately for us (unluckily for you), neither Indira Gandhi nor her Kashmiri *pandit* advisers understood economics. Her 'socialism' of populist slogans, nationalisations and intricate, energy-sapping controls of Indian industry, trade and investment kept your country poor and weak for 15 years. Her policies wrecked your textiles and other labour-using industries. It didn't even provide the mass education and healthcare that Mao had achieved for China. Our own leadership woke up to the developmental power of enterprise and markets by the late 1970s. It took your lot another dozen years. But, by then we had left you far behind. Even in the 1990s your approach to world trade and investment was so tentative. The brute fact is that in the last 15 years our per capita growth rate has been double yours and our annual increase in exports is more than your total exports! And almost half of India's children are malnourished (only a tenth in China). How can India be a competitor to China? We are in different leagues now.

SA: Aren't you exaggerating the disparities? What about our 8 per cent growth in the last 3 years? What about our great advances in IT and pharma? What about our burgeoning labour force? Every one talks about India's superior demographics.

MS (*thoughtfully*):...Interesting. My Politburo has been asking the same questions these last couple of years. But I told them not to worry. I gave them four big reasons why India will never rise to compete effectively with China. First, all this IT stuff is a sideshow, significant but a sideshow, nevertheless. Actually, IT usage and penetration in China is far more than in India. Even in IT exports, India's lead is temporary. Just compare after 5 years. Second, this 'superior demographics' argument is nonsense. It ignores India's huge failure to generate decent jobs. All those millions of new workers won't get real jobs; not as long as India persists with Indira Gandhi's inflexible labour laws. And India's illiterate (in economics) Left parties will block labour reforms for many more years. They can be relied upon to perpetuate casualisation and immiserisation of India's working class!

Third, India will never find either the resources or the will to build large-scale, quality infrastructure. Their politicians, 'babus' and pay commissions will always spend the bulk of public money on pay hikes for their tribe. And even if they found the money, their politico-administrative system has become so rickety, it simply lacks the capacity to decide and implement big projects successfully. Sloth, incompetence, political competition and corruption combine so effectively to block successful project execution. I showed my Politburo the latest reports of your Ministry of Programme Implementation, which demonstrate the huge time and cost over-runs on public projects.

Finally, I told them to watch how the quota/reservation debates and policies unfold. I predicted that this thoroughly bad approach to genuine problems of backwardness and inequity will spread in India, perhaps even to the private sector. And no society, which devalues merit and competence, can succeed in the modern world. Not to mention the massive social strife this policy will generate. The 8 per cent growth is only a temporary spurt. China need not worry about a truly 'resurgent India'. It's not going to happen.

SA (*gloomily*):... Thank you.

32

Talking Turkey

July has been the cruelest month. It started with another unseemly exercise of state power by the health minister against the director of the country's leading, government medical institution (and an outstanding cardiac surgeon). Just as people were wondering what authority the prime minister wielded over his cabinet colleague, the answer came, indirectly, through the speedy and humiliating reversal of his cabinet's decision to disinvest modest holdings of Nalco and Neyveli Lignite in the face of opposition from DMK 'allies'. Once again, the events demonstrated that real political power resides outside the PMO (this emperor is seriously underclad) and sparked editorials questioning the utility of such an 'anointed' PM. Meanwhile, in Mumbai, a few cloudbursts again showed up the massive infrastructure deficit in India's commercial capital. Much greater tragedy struck the 'maximum city' on 11th July, when eight bombs ripped through carriages of Mumbai's suburban trains, killing almost 200 innocent travellers and injuring many hundreds more. Preliminary investigations suggested the importance of home-grown terror networks, thriving in an ecology of weak governance and a compromised apparatus of law enforcement and justice. As if these very serious domestic setbacks to social harmony and development were not enough, the international environment worsened sharply. Massive Israeli overreaction to relatively minor Palestinian and Hezbollah provocations plunged the Middle East (especially Lebanon) into turmoil, sent oil prices above $ 75 a barrel and cast a shadow on global growth. The Doha round of trade negotiations staggered towards a possibly final breakdown without earning many column inches of global attention.

I could easily write a ponderous column on any one of these unhappy developments and depress myself and you (dear reader) in the bargain. Instead, I shall be escapist and talk about Turkey, where my wife and I spent a glorious fortnight last month. My reason (or excuse) for devoting scarce edit page space to a somewhat 'touristy' account is that we in India are woefully ignorant about Turkey, a remarkably successful, secular Muslim country of 70 million, located athwart the crossroads between Asia and Europe, with income per head of $ 4000 (as against $ 750 in India), an astonishingly diverse heritage (far better preserved than in India) and thoroughly modern aspirations for integration into Europe. Turkey does not merit such neglect.

The country is redolent with history. The Hittites ruled over most of Anatolia (roughly modern Turkey) from around 2000 BC to 1000 BC and sometimes clashed with the ambitions of Egyptian pharaohs. Displayed in Istanbul's Archaeological Museum (just next to Topkapi Palace) and carved on a stone tablet, is the world's oldest surviving peace treaty (of Kaddish), between Hittites and Egyptians in 1269 BC. In later centuries western Turkey was very much a part of the Hellenic golden age. Troy (or what little remains of it) is just across from the Gallipoli peninsula (where more than two millennia later, in 1915, young Winston Churchill helped develop the costly and abortive Allied campaign against Turko-German forces, including divisions led by another young man, Mustafa Kemal, later Ataturk, the indisputable founder of modern Turkey). The philosopher, Heraclaetus, was born around 540 BC in Ephesus in south-west Turkey. A few decades later the Greek historian, Herodotus, was growing up in nearby Bodrun. With the passage of centuries, the Greeks gave way to Romans, as in Ephesus, where the old Greek city (including the wondrous Temple of Artemis) has largely disappeared but the justly famous ruins of the Roman capital (of the province of Asia) still enthrall thousands of global tourists every day. By mid 4th century AD, Emperor Constantine had come to power and founded Constantinople (in his time called New Rome) as the capital of the Eastern Roman (or Byzantine) empire. In the 6th century, Justinian built the splendid Aya Sofia church, which even today is one of Istanbul's three most spectacular sights. As Byzantium went into decline around 1000 AD, power and territory was ceded to a medley of conquerors, including Selcuk Turks, Norman crusaders and Mongol hordes. The seeds of the Ottoman empire were sown in the early 14th century and flowered after Sultan Mehmet II conquered Constantinople in 1453. The empire reached its zenith in the 16th century under Suleyman the Magnificient, who greatly expanded the empire, decreed good laws, added major edifices to Constantinople, rebuilt Jerusalem and took Ottoman power to the gates of Vienna. After him came the long slow Ottoman decline to the 19th century 'sick man of Europe', which was only reversed after Ataturk took charge in 1923 and, almost single-handedly, invented modern Turkey.

Istanbul is steeped in this history. This magical 'city of a 1000 mosques' and 16 million people is criss-crossed by the Bosphorus and the Golden Horn and bounded on the south by the Sea of Marmara. Part of its immense appeal comes from the successful marriage of European standards of public infrastructure with Asian culture and hospitality (Istanbul meets my crucial test for successful modern cities...clean public toilets, a standard we don't even aspire to!). For sheer beauty of city centres there are few rivals in the world to the rose-bedecked park in Sultanahmet with the glorious Blue Mosque on one side and the majestic Aya Sofia on the other. For a contemplative afternoon, it's hard to beat the lovely gardens of the hill-top, Suleyman mosque (architect Sinan's masterpiece) from where you can gaze down on the Galata bridge spanning the Golden Horn to the posh Beyoglu district.

Turkey's charm is not limited to lovely mosques, churches and palaces. Geography has also been kind, lavishing the beautiful coastlines of the Aegean, Mediterranean and Black seas on three sides of the Anatolia peninsula. But for us the most spectacular scenery was the extraordinary moonscapes of Cappadocia in central Turkey, where millions-year-old volcanic ash sediments have eroded into thousands of conical rock outcrops (with phallic or mushroom shapes, 'depending on your perspective' as the Lonely Planet drily observes). Many of these 'fairy chimneys' were converted into dwellings in Hittite and Byzantine times (a growing number now host up-market pensions and mini-hotels!). Some of the larger conical outcrops were hollowed out into frescoed churches and monasteries in Byzantine years, as in Goreme.

With Muslims (mostly *Sunni*) accounting for 98 per cent of her population, you could call Turkey a Muslim country. But in practice it's a more secular nation than India. Kemal Ataturk's modernizing reforms of the 1920s have had a lasting impact. Today the Turkish gaze is firmly fixed on Europe and the goal of entry into the EU. (Even the ads on TV and hoardings display mainly blonde, Nordic models). In today's increasingly polarised world, Turkey's yearning is hardly reciprocated by the present EU membership. Yet, the 'Turkish way' could be the most effective antidote to the growing 'clash of civilizations'. The tragedy is that the chances of successful Turkish entry into the EU are clearly worse than even.

33

Foreign policy: mid-term report

Last month, I offered a somewhat rigorous assessment of the UPA government's economic policies over the past two and a half years (chap. 10). Someone (in PMO) asked whether I am ever complimentary to this government's policies. My answer is: of course, whenever the policies merit commendation. In foreign policy, they certainly do. Indeed, I would rate the government's foreign policy record as outstanding (if you want marks, a clear 80 per cent, may be higher). Let me elaborate.

What should be the framework of assessment? Well, as a rising 'middle power' with fairly serious long-term potential for a truly global role, India's current foreign policy priorities should be reasonably clear: strengthen strategic and economic ties with the world's sole superpower (while avoiding the Blairite fate of a 'yankee poodle'); improve relations with the rapidly ascending global power north of the Himalayas; pursue a delicate mix of amity and containment with nuclear-tipped and antagonistic Pakistan; deploy economic and political assets to promote peace and prosperity in South Asia; nurture the militarily significant and historically important ties with Eurasian Russia; foster good economic and political relations with other significant middle powers such as the 'big three' in Europe, Japan, Korea and ASEAN in Asia, and Brazil and Mexico in Latin America; and seek energy security, wherever possible.

Measured against this agenda, the UPA government has done very well. The strategic rapprochement with the US, launched so effectively by the predecessor NDA government, has been taken to a higher level. The pivotal 'nuclear deal' still hangs in the balance (of the US Congressional process and subsequent follow through), but to have got this far is quite an achievement for both sides, given the complexity of the issues and the thicket of cross-cutting interest groups and political alignments operating in both countries. On Pakistan too, Vajpayee may have taken the initial risks (and suffered the 'Kargil betrayal') but Manmohan Singh has also not hesitated to walk the mine-strewn path towards peace and normalisation with Pakistan. Whether his efforts can surmount the vested interest of large sections of the Pakistani state apparatus in a hostile stance towards India (not to mention the Indian political minefields of any compromise on Kashmir) remains to be seen. But high marks for trying.

Quiet diplomacy (again building on earlier initiatives) has kept the old border dispute with China from getting in the way of rapidly growing trade and investment between the two countries. High-level diplomacy has also nurtured Indo-Japanese relations away from the post-nuclear-tests freeze of 1998, to greener pastures and this healthy trend is likely to be reinforced by the next Prime Minister, Shinzo Abe. The political and defence-related ties with a resurgent Russia continue to be strong, though obviously not at pre-1990 levels. In the South Asian neighbourhood, Indian diplomacy contributed effectively to defusing the recent Nepal crisis, with significant (and uncharacteristic) help from the Left. In Sri Lanka, our policy has steadfastly supported the government of the day (and deepened bilateral economic ties), while gently encouraging a federal compromise with the secessionist LTTE. However, better relations with Bangladesh remain thwarted by the 'tribal' politics of that country and the unfortunate rise of fundamentalist forces. More generally, Indian policy has kicked the old habit of unproductive posturing on every international issue in preference for a more selective and focussed pursuit of priority national interests.

What explains the contrast between the government's consummate conduct of foreign policy and its weak record on economic policy? You might have expected the opposite with a world class economist as Prime Minister. There are several reasons. First, the Prime Minister has demonstrated exceptional (and unexpected) talent at personal diplomacy. His superior intelligence, dignity, sincerity and quiet humility, have been very effective with his counterpart leaders. Unlike several of his predecessors, he actually listens to his interlocutors and engages effectively in substantive discussions. He masters his briefs but is not imprisoned by them. When you think about it, we probably haven't had such a personable and wise conductor of prime ministerial dialogue with foreign leaders since Nehru (no, I am not looking for a job with PMO!). Indira Gandhi's unpredictable switches from charm to chill often disconcerted counterparts. Rajiv Gandhi's youthful enthusiasm and charm were infectious but, unlike Manmohan Singh, he did not always leave a lasting impression of great wisdom. And, in this domain, the other predecessors were just not in the same league, however powerful and politically popular they may have been.

Second, India happens to be in 'a sweet spot' in the evolution of geopolitics. The combination of a quarter of a century of economic growth at six per cent a year, demonstrated nuclear capability and a billion plus population has at last made the country a non-trivial player in the global sweepstakes. The unprecedented surge of China's economic and political power has encouraged quite a few countries to look for explicit or implicit counterweights in global *realpolitik*. For some, India seems to fit the bill. Third, unlike domestic economic policy, which is all too often held hostage to the interplay of ideologies, entrenched interests and shifting political alliances, the conduct of foreign policy is mostly left to the professionals, with political guidance from the Prime Minister, the Foreign Minister (when we have one) and, of course, Sonia Gandhi. Exceptions are there, of course, such as Pakistan (always) and one-off issues like the US-India nuclear deal, when everybody (and their aunt!) gets into the fray. But these are exceptions, which the Prime Minister and his national security establishment have handled with much skill...thus far.

Finally, the UPA government has been fortunate in having Shyam Saran to oversee the MEA establishment during this period (no, he is not a personal buddy). By nearly all accounts, he has handled the varied challenges of foreign secretaryship (ranging from being the point man on the nuclear deal with the US to handling the occasional delinquent envoy in some distant land) with much intelligence, aplomb and professionalism. (There must have been rather special and peculiar challenges when his minister slipped on an oil slick a year ago and 'went ballistic' on national TV). Nor has Saran fallen prey to the temptation of seeking personal publicity, giving interviews only when the occasion really required it. It's a pity he couldn't be persuaded to stay on for a year, especially since that might have avoided the patent unhappiness of senior IFS officers caused by the transition to the indubitably able (but not quite so senior) Shiv Shankar Menon.

In closing, and to paraphrase the title of a recent hit movie, good night Shyam and good luck Shankar!

Sources

CHAPTER NO. / TITLE / SOURCE

1. India's economy: then and now
   Outlook, April 4, 2005.
2. Can India grow without *Bharat*?
   Business Standard, November 25, 2003.
3. Guaranteeing employment or fiscal crisis?
   Business Standard, November 30, 2004.
4. Reviving industrial employment
   Business Standard, November 22, 2005.
5. Why did India reform?
   Business Standard, February 24, 2004.
6. Reforms, may be but at what speed?
   Business Standard, May 25, 2004.
7. Bad ideas *versus* good men
   Business Standard, June 22, 2004.
8. Bad ideas are winning
   Business Standard, December 28, 2004.
9. Populism rides again
   Business Standard, December 27, 2005.
10. Economic policy: mid-term report
    Business Standard, August 22, 2006.
11. What is happening in services?
    Business Standard, December 23, 2003.
12. Growth prospects: a reality check
    Business Standard, April 27, 2004.

13. Eight per cent growth forever?
Business Standard, May 23, 2006.

14. Foreign exchange for infrastructure, anyone?
Business Standard, October 26, 2004.

15. A tale of three cities
Business Standard, August 23, 2005.

16. India's water troubles
Business Standard, October 24, 2005.

17. The good, the bad and the ugly
Business Standard, January 30, 2004.

18. Tax policies for 2005
Business Standard, January 25, 2005.

19. India's tax reformers
Business Standard, April 26, 2005.

20. The year of bad taxes
Business Standard, January 24, 2006.

21. A curate's egg
Business Standard, March 8, 2006.

22. Wanted: A trade policy
Business Standard, September 23, 2003.

23. The ABC of PTAs and FTAs
Business Standard, October 28, 2003.

24. A common currency for SAARC?
Business Standard, August 24, 2004.

25. A new BoP paradigm?
Business Standard, February 22, 2005.

26. Global imbalances
Business Standard, October 24, 2006.

27. Inflation and monetary policy
Business Standard, September 28, 2004.

28. Farewell fiscal responsibility?
Business Standard, March 22, 2005.

29. Fiscal deficit, what's that?
Business Standard, November 30, 2006.

30. Not in China's league
Business Standard, September 27, 2005.

31. China's India strategy
Business Standard, May 9, 2006.

32. Talking Turkey
Business Standard, July 25, 2006.

33. Foreign policy: mid-term report
Business Standard, September 26, 2006.